YOU AND THE HOLY SPIRIT

You

and the Holy Spirit

A NEGLECTED NEW TESTAMENT DOCTRINE
MADE PERSONAL AND PRACTICAL FOR EVERYDAY LIFE

by Stuart R. Oglesby

JOHN KNOX PRESS

RICHMOND, VIRGINIA

Other books by Stuart R. Oglesby

BECOMING A MEMBER OF THE PRESBYTERIAN CHURCH

PRAYERS FOR ALL OCCASIONS

PRESBYTERIANISM IN ACTION

WHAT IS YOUR NEED?

THE BABY IS BAPTIZED

THINK ON THESE THINGS

231.3

Og 5y

36325

March 1958

Preface

The chapters which this book contains do not present a definitive study of the Christian doctrine of the Holy Spirit. Rather, they attempt to bring a neglected and essential New Testament teaching down into the everyday lives of church members who have felt a lack of satisfaction and peace in their Christian experience, the need for more wisdom in dealing with the problems of life, and the sadness of their failure to exert a saving influence on the lives of many with whom they come into daily contact.

There is no claim made for originality in what is written. The writer humbly and gratefully acknowledges his indebtedness to many teachers and authors who have contributed over a long period of years to his understanding of the practical value of the work and influence of the Holy Spirit. Growing out of postgraduate study of the doctrine of Pneumatology in Union Theological Seminary in Virginia, the material in this book has been preached many times over during a pastorate of more than twenty years in Central Presbyterian Church in Atlanta, Georgia.

Encouraged by the appreciation and interest of members of his congregation, the writer trusts that these twelve expositions of the doctrine of the Third Person of the Trinity may have value for a wider group in the Church at large.

STUART R. OGLESBY
Atlanta, Georgia

Contents

Contents

YOU AND THE HOLY SPIRIT

Chapter 1

THE SPIRIT OF GOD
AND THE SONS OF GOD

"For as many as are led by the Spirit of God, they are the sons of God." — ROMANS 8:14.

THERE ARE TOO MANY PEOPLE who seem to be unwilling to accept any doctrine of Christian faith which they are not able to understand. Such an attitude is foolish, because Christianity is either a supernatural, revealed religion, or it is only one among many ethnic religions of the world. As a matter of fact, there is not one ordinary thing even in secular life which a man can completely understand. Tennyson sets forth this fact in a familiar stanza:

"Flower in the crannied wall,
I pluck you out of the crannies,
I hold you here, root and all, in my hand,
Little flower — but if I could understand
What you are, root and all, and all in all,
I should know what God and man is."[1]

There is another and much larger group of people who seem willing to believe and accept anything in religion that is weird, fantastic, unusual, or contrary to human reason. This is a residue heritage of superstition which is hard to get rid of. It brings no honor to Christianity and it does no credit to Christians. It confuses credulity with faith, childishness with childlikeness, sentimentalism with a deep religious motivation.

The Christian doctrine of the Trinity is a doctrine hard to understand aright. The doctrine of the Holy Spirit is a doctrine hard for Christians to receive, believe, and hold without their slipping into religious vagaries which do harm to the cause of Christ. In this chapter I shall not speak of the doctrine of the Trinity as such, nor attempt to consider the doctrine of the Holy Spirit in its entirety. Instead, I want you to think of what Paul meant when he said, "For as many as are led by the Spirit of God, they are the sons of God."

The Law of the Spirit of Life

In the eighth chapter of Romans the Holy Spirit, in distinction from the regenerate human spirit, is mentioned ten times: The Spirit (v. 1); Spirit of life (v. 2); Spirit of God (vv. 9, 14); Spirit of Christ (v. 9); Spirit that raised Christ (v. 11); Spirit that indwells (v. 11); Spirit that witnesses (v. 16); Spirit having first fruits (v. 23); Spirit that helps (v. 26); Spirit that intercedes (vv. 26-27).

The expression "law of the Spirit of life" means the effective, working principle of spiritual life as contrasted with the working principle of sin and death which is found in man in his natural condition. Paul is clearly speaking of the work of the Holy Spirit as the Third Person of the Trinity when he uses this phrase. This principle of divine life is neither self-originated nor self-sustained. It is a part of the redemptive work of God, carried on by His Holy Spirit.

In order for a sinful man's life to be led and guided by the Spirit of God there must first be a work of divine grace in his heart. This work of grace begins with a new birth, which we call Regeneration. "Ye must be born again" — or, "from above." The new birth is entirely a work of God's Spirit without any part of it being done, or accomplished, by man himself. Two great systems of religious thought part company here. One of them holds that man must co-operate in the work of regeneration. Using the illustration of a drowning man, the advocates of this system hold that he must at least climb up on whatever raft, or piece of timber, or mound of rock there may be near him in the raging torrent, and that God, seeing his distressed earnestness, will then lift him completely out of danger. The other system holds that God does all the rescuing without any climbing to safety on the part of man being necessary or even possible. A drowning man is helpless. One dead in trespasses and sins cannot even catch hold of a lifeline thrown to him.

At the same time, Scripture teaches that the new birth is given to man in response to repentance and faith, both of which are "saving graces" bestowed upon man as gracious gifts. "By grace are ye saved through faith; and that not of yourselves: it is the gift of God." (Ephesians 2:8.) The Westminster Shorter Catechism definitions of faith and of repentance are helpful here. In answer to the question, "What is repentance unto life?" the answer is: "Repentance unto life is a saving grace, whereby a sinner, out of a true sense of his sin, and apprehension of the mercy of God in Christ, doth, with grief and hatred of his sin, turn from it unto God, with full purpose of, and endeavor after, new obedience." The question, "What is faith in Jesus Christ?" has the answer: "Faith in Jesus Christ is a saving grace, whereby we receive and rest upon Him alone for salvation, as He is offered to us in the gospel."

The new birth is, therefore, the implanting of a new principle of life in the heart of man. When he has been born again he is a "babe in Christ," with all his growth and development, his service and sacrifice, before him. He must, from then on, continually grow in grace and in the knowledge of our Lord and Saviour. The evidences of a new birth are found in the growth and development which take place in the heart and life of a Christian. There is no conclusive proof save these. And since growth and development are often slow and retarded they may never provide a conclusive proof, certainly not in every case. What is a man to do then if he feels worried about his regeneration and longs for a better evidence than his life supplies him?

A negative answer to this question may first be in order. Our feelings have nothing to do with the matter, being neither an evidence for nor against the fact of a new birth. It is significant that the New Testament has so little to say about our feelings, and strange that Christians have made so much of them as evidences. A theologian would say: "Assurance of salvation is not of the essence of saving faith." That just means that a person does not have to feel he is saved in order to be saved. John, in his Epistle, puts it thus: "If our heart condemn us, God is greater than our heart, and knoweth all things." (I John 3:20.)

A positive answer might be given in the words of Job: "Though he slay me, yet will I trust in him." (Job 13:15.) Or even better, in the words of David Livingstone, who, in the midst of his trials and sufferings in Africa, stayed himself on the parting words of Jesus: "Lo, I am with you alway." Said he, "It is the word of a Gentleman of the most strict and sacred honor, so there's an end to it." On that pledge, he hazarded his all. And it did not fail him. Better still, in the words of Jesus: "Him that cometh to me I will in no wise cast out." (John 6:37.) So there's an end to it! "The law [or principle] of the Spirit of life in Christ Jesus hath made me free from the law [or principle] of sin and death." (Romans 8:2.)

The Sons of God

There is a sense in which all men are the sons of God. They come fresh from His creative hands. They are brethren because they are all descendants of the first man created. "God created man in his own image, in the image of God created he him; male and female created he them." (Genesis 1:27.) When a new life is born into the world, it is not a new creation. Rather, it is a reproduction. Therefore, there is a real sense in which we may speak of man's universal brotherhood.

Christian sonship and Christian brotherhood is a very different thing from natural sonship and natural brotherhood. When the

Holy Spirit changes the heart of a sinful man, He convinces him of his sin and misery, enlightens his mind in the knowledge of Christ, renews his will, and enables him to embrace Jesus Christ freely offered to him in the Gospel. Such a man is then "united with Christ," received into the family of God, and has a right to all the privileges of the sons of God. "Behold, what manner of love the Father hath bestowed upon us, that we should be called the sons of God." (I John 3:1.)

When God receives a man into His family as a son, He forgives his sins and gives him a new standing, or a new status, in life. This pardon and this new standing are the result of the work of Christ, the Saviour of sinners. Because of Christ's death, God pardons our sins. Because of Christ's resurrection, God clothes us with a righteousness which is not our own but is provided for us by God's Son. This is called in theological terms, Justification.

Being adopted into the family of God, Christian men and women are from henceforth "led" by the Spirit of God in growth and development in the Christian life. This growth and development is called Sanctification, a work of the Spirit which enables believers in Christ more and more to die unto sin and live unto righteousness.

Christian sonship (being led by the Spirit of God) means first of all that a former rebellious sinner has been brought into fellowship with God, and into harmony with God's character and purposes. Sinful things which formerly brought pleasure no longer do so, and spiritual things which seemed before to be foolishness are now seen as wisdom, mercy, and power. A son may not understand, or even appreciate, all his father does, but being in harmony with him and devoted to him, he accepts these things as best. So a spiritual son of the Most High believes where he cannot prove and trusts God when he cannot see the end of the way he is being led. "It doth not yet appear what we shall be: but we know that, when he shall appear, we shall be like him; for we shall see him as he is." (I John 3:2.)

A spiritual son of God is the object of his Father's peculiar affection. God loves all men, but He loves His sons with a different kind of love from that which He bestows on men in general. The two types of love are easily distinguished in the Greek New Testament, for two entirely different words are used.

There is no power like that of genuine and pure love for bringing out the best that is in man. It acts like the sun bringing forth the beauty and fragrance of flowers. "Love," said Henry Drummond in a famous sermon, "is the greatest thing in the world." It is indeed the greatest thing in this world and also in the world to come. It is the greatest purifier of life, the greatest inspiration to noble action, and the greatest producer of faith which is the victory that overcomes the world. "God so loved the world, that he gave his only begotten Son, that whosoever believeth in him should not perish, but have everlasting life." No wonder this verse is called the golden text of the Bible.

A son is entitled to certain privileges in the household to which he belongs. So is a spiritual son in the Household of God. These privileges are too many to be enumerated, but they may all be summed up under the terms (1) consecration, (2) companionship, (3) confidence.

Men dedicate themselves to the service of God, and God then consecrates them. We may confidently expect an answer to the prayer of the familiar hymn: "Consecrate me now to Thy service, Lord." When God consecrates a man, He bestows upon him all the powers necessary for his growth in grace. He supplies every need out of His rich, unfailing storehouse of mercy.

Companionship in life is the second gift of God to His sons. Men are lonely as they travel along through the years, no matter how many people may be around them. There is an inner, secret center of life into which no friend, however close, may find entrance. The Divine Friend can and does enter there, and His Presence brings joy unspeakable and full of glory. "I've found a Friend, oh, such a Friend," a well-known hymn puts it. This is good though not entirely true, for it is the Friend who has found me. As Pascal so well said: "I would not now be seeking Thee, if Thou had'st not already found me."

Confidence in the face of all that opposes us, or would make us afraid, is another blessing that comes to the sons of God. So Paul wrote: "I can do all things through Christ which strengtheneth me." (Philippians 4:13.) He seems to be saying: "Life, bring me what you will, I am sufficient, ready, and prepared."

Let me close this chapter with the warning with which it began. Be careful not to reject the things in your religion you cannot understand. The sons of God must live by faith and not by sight. At the same time be careful lest great Christian truths lead you into something that is sub-Christian. All the work of the Holy Spirit in the heart of a man takes place in the unity of a single self-consciousness. "The human spirit is not conscious of the Divine Spirit, as of an agent other than and distinct from himself. That is religious enthusiasm in the bad sense. . . . The believer would not have known that there is another person than himself concerned in this confident personal assurance of adoption [into the family of God as a son], had it not been taught to him. . . . The witness of the Spirit is not a doctrine of psychology, but of revelation."[2] This quotation from Shedd's Commentary on Romans sounds a warning that was never needed more than it is today.

"For as many as are led by the Spirit of God, they are the sons of God." What and who are in control of the direction of your life?

Chapter 2

THE HOLY SPIRIT AT WORK

"And when he [the Spirit] is come, he will reprove the world of sin, and of righteousness, and of judgment." — JOHN 16:8.

THE PERSON AND WORK of the Holy Spirit is necessarily a mysterious doctrine. Being spiritual and thus unseen, intangible and secret, the power of the Spirit can never be perfectly understood by mortal man. Nevertheless, there are certain facts concerning the Spirit and His work which are set forth plainly in the Bible. If Christians understood these facts better they would be saved from many of the strange developments in religion which have grown up around this doctrine, and the doctrine itself would become more inspiring and strengthening.

To many evangelical Christians, to whom Christ is an abiding and living reality, the Spirit is only a name for a more or less vague influence and power. Surely, this should not be true. The Spirit can and should become a real person, a vital influence, an abiding reality, to earnest Christians who seek to know Him and to understand His work.

It must have been a startling announcement that Jesus made to His disciples when He told them, near the close of His life, that it was expedient, or best, for Him to go away. In order to understand the consternation which the announcement caused, let us think back through the centuries and try to picture the little huddled group of men in the upper room where Jesus was having His last heart-to-heart talk with them. They were already fearful and confused at the way things were going. Very little understanding faith had developed in them during the time of their association with the Master. They faced a world that was cruel and hostile. Like frightened children they clung to the person of Jesus. Yet He said it was best that He go away and leave them. Then He patiently and sympathetically tried to explain what He meant.

Our words of Christian resignation at the death of one beloved, "It was for the best," bear no analogy to the words of Jesus concerning His departure from the world and from His followers. The coming of the Spirit awaited the departure of Jesus. "It is expedient for you that I go away: for if I go not away, the Comforter will not come unto you; but if I depart, I will send him unto you." (John 16:7.) The death, burial, resurrection, and ascension of our blessed Lord must be accomplished before the Spirit could enter into His distinctive ministry. When the work on earth of the incarnated Christ was completed, then — and not until then — would the work on earth of the Holy Spirit begin.

Jesus accepted the limitations of humanity when He came to earth. The Holy Spirit would not be subject to these limitations. He would work within the hearts of believers; whereas Jesus had to teach them from without, as one man teaching another. The Spirit would not be limited by time or space. The incarnated Christ of necessity could only be in one place at a time; whereas the Spirit would be able to work when, and where, and how He chose, touching the hearts of men in different places at the same time. Being God, Himself, He would be omnipotent and omnipresent. Thus He would be able to make possible the fulfillment of those strange words of Jesus: "He that believeth on me, the works that I do shall he do also; and greater works than these shall he do; because I go unto my Father." (John 14:12.)

People often look back yearningly to the time when Christ was on earth, and feel that if He were here today all would be well. I do not believe that would be any truer now than it was in the days of long ago. Surely, unless we are completely deceived, He knew what was best for His disciples then, as well as for His disciples now. And He said it was best for Him to go so that the Spirit of Truth, the Comforter, might come. The Spirit did come on the Day of Pentecost and has been carrying on His distinctive work in the world and in the hearts of believers ever since that memorable day. Therefore, we have lost nothing that the Apostles had which was worth keeping, and we have gained much that they had not.

The work of the Holy Spirit in the world is set forth in these words of Jesus: "And when he is come, he will reprove the world of sin, and of righteousness, and of judgment." (John 16:8.) The word for "reprove" is better translated "convict," or "convinced." The work of the Holy Spirit in the world is three-fold — convicting, or convincing, men of sin, of righteousness, and of judgment. This is not always, or necessarily, a saving conviction but is a preliminary work which in the case of some will lead to salvation, but in the case of others will not be effective. Not in the work of salvation but rather in the work of conviction has the Old Testament prophecy been fulfilled that the Spirit of God should be poured out upon all flesh.

Conviction of Sin

The first work of the Holy Spirit in the world is to convict men of sin. It is an outstanding characteristic of the message of the Gospel that it emphasizes first of all the terrible reality of sin and the inevitability of its consequences. The wages of sin is death, and the fact of sin colors and conditions every experience of man. It has been said that all the problems of the world can be reduced to two — the existence of sin and how man can be freed from its power and pollution. But mankind remains ignorant of the true nature of sin, or indifferent to it, until a conviction is wrought by the Holy Spirit. A pseudo-Christianity which does not build on such a conviction is impotent, and incapable of meeting the needs of sinful men. A religion which neglects the fact of sin cannot last very long, for it is only a sham at its best and a mocking deceiver at its worst.

Christianity is more than a beautiful system of ethics — Confucianism is that. It is more than a guide of life — Buddhism claims to be that. It is more than a revelation of truth — Mohammedanism professes to reveal divine truth. It is a redemptive power from sin, and man cannot be redeemed from that in which he does not believe, of which he is not convicted. Here, then, is the first work of the Spirit — to reveal to man the exceeding sinfulness of sin, its bondage and awful consequences, and to convict man as a sinner.

Mankind naturally does not like to face the fact of sin. Men are prone to speak of their failings as physical weaknesses or psychological complexes. This is the result of man's pride, and pride of heart and life is itself the primary sin as well as the root of all sin. The Spirit convicts men of the sin of pride, reveals what the nature of sin is, and makes men hate sin by holding up the one supreme example of its diabolical work, the crucifixion of Christ. "He shall convict the world of sin, because they believed not on me." (See John 16:8-9.) That is what sin did, the sin of unbelief followed by a train of inevitable consequences.

When Peter preached his great sermon to the assembled multitude on the Day of Pentecost, he did not soften his charge of sin. "Ye men of Israel, hear these words; Jesus of Nazareth, a man approved of God among you by miracles and wonders and signs, which God did by him in the midst of you, as ye yourselves also know: him . . . ye have taken, and by wicked hands have crucified and slain." (Acts 2:22-23.) It was then that the Holy Spirit, just now beginning His peculiar work in God's plan of redemption, wrought conviction in the hearts of those who heard and they cried out: "Men and brethren, what shall we do?" So it is today that when men are convicted of the sin of unbelief on Jesus, they can for the first time see the true nature and consequences of all sin. The sin which crucified Jesus is the sin that is abroad in the world of our day, and the Holy Spirit is still carrying on His work of conviction, "when, and where, and how He pleaseth."[3]

CONVICTION OF RIGHTEOUSNESS

The conviction of righteousness comes after the conviction of sin. There is little use of offering healing to a man who does not know he is sick. Preaching the love of God to one who does not realize that his sin has separated him from God will not make much of an impression. It is useless to ask a man to be saved when he does not believe himself to be lost. But a conviction of sin, standing alone, would drive a man to despair. After being convicted of sin, he is then ready for a conviction of righteousness. The question is, where and how can righteousness be found? You had just as well command a sponge not to absorb water into which it has been dropped as to order a natural man in this world of sin not to be a sinner. Jesus told His disciples: "Except your righteousness shall exceed the righteousness of the scribes and Pharisees, ye shall in no case enter into the kingdom of heaven." (Matthew 5:20.) But how can it? Many of the scribes and Pharisees earnestly tried to live up to the best they knew, but it was not enough.

The conviction of righteousness goes further than a conviction of the need of righteousness. The Holy Spirit, after convicting a man of the need of righteousness, convinces him of the existence of a righteousness God has provided and made available to him. Again, just as the conviction of sin is not always a saving conviction, so the conviction of righteousness does not always bring righteousness into the possession of one convinced of its existence. Still further work of the Spirit is necessary in the heart of a man convicted of sin before it becomes a saving conviction, and likewise further work of the Spirit is necessary before a man convicted of his need for righteousness and its existence can claim that righteousness as his own.

What is this righteousness, of which the Spirit brings conviction? The Scriptural answer to this question is that it is a righteousness of God and not a righteousness that man himself can work out. Paul said that he counted all his best efforts towards attaining righteousness as worse than nothing, but that his hope was to obtain the righteousness of God which comes through faith in Christ. (Philippians 3:8-9.) The conviction of righteousness which the Holy Spirit alone can place in the heart of a man is that God has provided a righteousness in the person and work of His Son and that this is made available for sinful man if and when he has faith to claim it.

"When He shall come with trumpet sound,
Oh, may I then in Him be found,
Clothed in His righteousness alone,
Faultless to stand before the throne."[4]

"He will convict the world . . . of righteousness, because I go to my Father, and ye see me no more." (See John 16:8, 10.)

The return of Christ to His Father in heaven marked the completion of our Saviour's work on earth and, at the same time, provided proof that His mission had been successful. A dead Christ, lying in some tomb forgotten and neglected, or even remembered and praised, could have no power to change the lives of men. A Christ whose work had been gloriously accomplished, who had proven Himself to be the conqueror of death and hell, could send forth from heaven to which He had returned the Holy Spirit to bring conviction to men of a righteousness which He had worked out and made available for them on the condition of faith.

"My hope is built on nothing less
Than Jesus' blood and righteousness."

CONVICTION OF JUDGMENT

When sin and righteousness meet in the world there is always conflict between them. "What fellowship hath righteousness with unrighteousness? and what communion hath light with darkness?" (II Corinthians 6:14.) The result of the conflict is judgment, and the stronger will prevail.

There is a judgment being made each day in the world and in the life of every man. Righteousness and unrighteousness are continually striving for superiority. Every choice a man makes, every word he speaks, every act he performs, involves a judgment. The Holy Spirit makes plain to men of the world what sin is, so that they are without excuse. He then reveals what righteousness is, where it may be found, and how it may be gained. A choice between sin and righteousness then must be made. A failure to choose righteousness is a decision against it and a decision in favor of sin.

> ". . . . to every man there openeth
> A High Way and a Low,
> And every man decideth
> The Way his soul shall go."[5]

The supreme example of judgment which the Holy Spirit uses in the matter of conviction of judgment is that the prince of this world has already been judged and condemned. "He shall convict the world . . . of judgment, because the prince of this world is judged." (See John 16:8, 11.) This is purely a matter of divine revelation for, according to outward appearances, the Devil is still very much alive in the world and very active in the affairs of men. But he is only loosed for a little while, a definite period of time, and his ultimate destruction is assured. When Jesus cried on the cross, "It is finished," the doom of Satan was sealed; the victory of righteousness was made not only possible but inevitable.

There is a further truth regarding judgment which comes to us from the words of Jesus. Not only is there a judgment going on, day by day, but there is in the future a last and final judgment. The Judgment Day, of which people speak sometimes carelessly and jokingly, will be very real. If I do not make friends with and ally myself with the divine righteousness which is offered me here and now, I shall one day have to confront it with fear and trembling in the other world. The judgment which follows a rejection of Christ on earth is irrevocable and final. Therefore, in the words of Jesus we should read a warning — a loving, pleading warning, but a warning which holds out no hope of repentance and a change of heart after death.

Here, then, is the threefold conviction which no man can afford to neglect — of sin which is mine, of righteousness which may be mine, and of judgment which must be mine. The Gospel is a "savour of life unto life," or a "savour of death unto death." (See II Corinthians 2:16.) Men are either saved by a proclamation of divine mercy and grace, or they are left without excuse. This is the work of the Holy Spirit in the world.

Chapter 3

WITNESS THAT ASSURES

"The Spirit itself beareth witness with our spirit, that we are the children of God." — ROMANS 8:16.

Is IT POSSIBLE for Christians to be assured in their hearts that God has accepted them as His sons? Can a man ever become certain that he is saved? Well, such a thing is possible but it is not always actually so. It may be that it is not even frequently so. Perhaps this is just as well, for too much assurance could easily retard the progress of a believer in his growth in grace. We know that sometimes those who seem to be most certain about their salvation appear to give little evidence of the fact in the spirit they manifest and in the attitudes they assume. However, a better understanding of the witness of the Holy Spirit to our sonship would enable us to grow daily into a more satisfying assurance, one that is satisfying to ourselves without being offensive to others.

As he writes the comforting truth about the witness of the Spirit, Paul is preparing to ascend to the heights in the latter portion of the eighth chapter of Romans, which has been aptly called "the sunlit summit of the Christian Gospel." No man can go with him all the way to the top without some assurance that he is a child of God. Before making the climb, therefore, Paul points out how such an assurance may be obtained.

THE WITNESS IS WITHIN

Reserving until later that to which witness is borne, let us note first that the Spirit's testimony and convincing work is within the heart of a Christian. It is a distinctive characteristic of the ministry of the Holy Spirit that He touches the deep places in the spirit of man. "What man knoweth the things of a man, save the spirit of man which is in him?" (I Corinthians 2:11.)

As a boy, while sitting in church and apparently listening to the sermon, I would sometimes let my thoughts and imagination wander uncontrolled. Who has not been guilty of the same thing, not only as a boy but also in later life? One imaginative event so intrigued me that it reappeared often in my mind. It was that some miraculous happening was about to occur which would prove that my denomination was right and all others wrong. That was in the days of rather intense denominational antagonisms. I could see a great slab of marble falling from heaven, crashing through the roof of the church, and coming to rest just in front of the pulpit. On this marble slab, chiseled by the hand of God, was an inscription which was intended to bring joy and triumph to the hearts of Presbyterians, and terror to the hearts of all others. Certainly this is an utterly ridiculous example of wishful thinking of an immature mind, but it may be permissible to use it as an illustration of the spiritually immature desire of man for some startling, external proof of the truth of his religion, as well as an external authority to which he can yield without the trouble of disciplining his mind and controlling his spirit.

Let us think of some of the things the Lord might have done to save the world, and some of the methods He might have used, but did not. He could have been incarnated as a mighty and victorious king, rather than as a helpless babe. He could have destroyed all His enemies and exalted His friends instead of living as a humble servant and helper of mankind. He could have lived in a palace instead of having no place to lay His head. He could have established and completed immediately a great earthly kingdom instead of merely laying the foundations of a spiritual Kingdom within the hearts of a handful of believers. Surely we would have handled the matter differently if it had been left to us. We can now see and understand that a display of supernatural force might have secured the outward allegiance of many people, but would never have been effective in disciplining their spirits and making their hearts pure. Or can we?

Pursuing the thought further, Jesus could have left for the instruction of believers authoritative writings of His own, He could have set up a great and skillfully organized church, He could have laid down infallible rules for everything that life then contained and was to develop later. Yet, so far as the record goes, He did not write anything, save that unforgettable writing with His finger on the sand the day the Pharisees tried to force Him to condemn a woman taken in sin. He organized no church and gave no instructions about the future organization and work of His Church. He did not even speak of the method of baptism, about which so much has been spoken and written since His time. He seemed to be content with planting seeds of truth within the hearts of His followers and of leaving the details of putting these truths into operation to be worked out by Christians when the time came. They were not to do this unaided and undirected, for He promised that the Holy Spirit would guide men into all truth and, by implication, would also guide them in the use of methods for implementing truth.

There are Christian people now, and doubtless always will be, who set external authority over the internal witness of the Spirit. They try to bring others into subjection to an authority which is in accordance with their own ideas and interpretations, or that of the group to which they belong. Their contention is that such subjection is necessary in the interests of uniformity, orthodoxy, and even of salvation itself. The authority of the Church, like the authority of the Spirit, must always be an inner authority. To set up an external, final authority of any kind over a Christian is to travel on the road which leads ultimately and logically to the Roman Catholic Church and to the doctrine of papal infallibility.

The Spirit of God and the Spirit of Man

While the witness of the Holy Spirit is within the hearts of men, it does not override the natural functions and working of the human spirit. It is not a trance, a vision, or an ecstatic dream. Rather, it is a work of purifying the believer's own spirit, strengthening him in his Christian faith, and causing him to grow in the assurance that he is a true child of God.

> "I ask no dream, no prophet ecstasies,
> No sudden rending of the veil of clay,
> No angel visitant, no opening skies;
> But take the dimness of my soul away."[6]

Human spirits are subject to human frailties. Men are often depressed in spirit, disturbed and uncertain. "Sometimes I'm up and sometimes I'm down," describes the condition of every human heart. It is a natural human tendency to think that prosperity indicates the favor of God, while adversity shows lack of divine favor. If the Old Testament seems at times to encourage this belief, the New Testament, with its fuller revelation of God's character and purposes, very plainly discourages it and seeks to banish it from the thinking of believers.

A brief résumé of the teachings of Jesus and the New Testament writers on the subject of the experiences of Christians in their contact with the world ought to be sufficient to set us straight in our thinking about this matter. The two concluding "beatitudes" of the Sermon on the Mount are in point: "Blessed are they which are persecuted for righteousness' sake: for their's is the kingdom of heaven. Blessed are ye, when men shall revile you, and persecute you, and shall say all manner of evil against you falsely, for my sake. Rejoice, and be exceeding glad: for great is your reward in heaven." (Matthew 5:10-12.) In His last intimate talk with His disciples just before His arrest, Jesus warned them that in the world they should have tribulation. "But," He added, "be of good cheer; I have overcome the world." (John 16:33.) The Apostle Paul, writing to Timothy, reminded his young disciple of the persecutions and afflictions which had been his lot as a missionary to the Gentiles, and added: "Yea, and all that will live godly in Christ Jesus shall suffer persecution." (II Timothy 3:12.) The writer to the Hebrews gave this wholesome admonition which seems to be addressed to us individually today: "My son, despise not thou the chastening of the Lord, nor faint when thou art rebuked of him: for whom the Lord loveth he chasteneth, and scourgeth every son whom he receiveth." (Hebrews 12:5-6.) James seems to sum up the whole matter in these words: "My brethren, count it all joy when ye fall into divers temptations; knowing this, that the trying of your faith worketh patience. But let patience have her perfect work, that ye may be perfect and entire, wanting nothing." (James 1:2-4.)

The witness of the Spirit with our spirits takes away the doubts and fears which adversity brings, and applies to our hearts such truths as have just been quoted. The Spirit assures and convinces us that God has many loving and wise ways of dealing with His children and that prosperity is not always one of these. It is the Spirit who teaches men how to rejoice in tribulation.

Just as it is impossible to chart the working of a human spirit, so it is impossible to define or even to understand fully the means and methods used by the Holy Spirit in His work of witnessing to our spirits. As the wind bloweth where it listeth, and thou canst not tell whence it cometh or whither it goeth, to use Jesus' own illustration, so the witness of the Holy Spirit mysteriously steals into our hearts, bringing an increasing assurance that we are children of God. This assurance is able to stand up against inner feelings of guilt, or of doubt, and against outward experiences of trouble and sorrow.

> "Should Thy mercy send me
>   Sorrow, toil, and woe,
> Or should pain attend me
>   On my path below,
> Grant that I may never
>   Fail Thy hand to see:
> Grant that I may ever
>   Cast my care on Thee."[7]

THE WITNESS TO SONSHIP

The witness that the Holy Spirit bears to the spirit of a redeemed man is to the fact of his sonship. This special work of the Spirit should not be confused with regeneration, for the work of regeneration, being born again, must have been completed before a man can become a child of God. Certainly, the Spirit would not bear false witness in the heart of an unregenerate sinner. The witness of the Spirit, coming after the new birth, is given to assure a believer that he has already become a member of the family of God. "As many as received him [Jesus], to them gave he power* to become the sons of God, even to them that believe on his name." (John 1:12.)

In the verse immediately preceding the good news of the witness of the Spirit, Paul wrote: "Ye have not received the spirit of bondage again to fear; but ye have received the spirit of adoption, whereby we cry, Abba, Father." (Romans 8:15.) The spirit of bondage and of fear is the common lot of those on the outside of the family of God. A son, however, has the right and privilege of calling God, "Abba, Father," and in his new-found confidence is released from the spirit of bondage into the glorious freedom of the sons of God.

The expression "Abba, Father" is found three times in the New Testament. In Mark 14:36 Jesus, Himself, used the words while He was praying in the Garden of Gethsemane. "Abba, Father, all things are possible unto thee; take away this cup from me: nevertheless not what I will, but what thou wilt." In Galatians 4:6 it is stated that the Spirit cries, "Abba, Father." "Because ye are sons, God hath sent forth the Spirit of his Son into your hearts, crying, Abba, Father." In Romans 8:15, the believer himself is said to use the endearing term. "For ye have not received the spirit of bondage again to fear; but ye have received the Spirit of adoption, whereby we cry, Abba, Father."

The word "Abba" is Aramaic for the Hebrew word meaning Father. While Hebrew was still used in synagogues and schools at the time of Jesus, Aramaic was the vernacular of Palestine, the

---

*Or "the right," as in American Standard Version.

language the people used in their everyday life. Jesus and the Apostles all spoke Aramaic. Since it was the language of the home, it was the language of the heart. Dr. Charles Hodge in his commentary on Romans makes this interesting observation: "It is rare, indeed, that any other than our mother tongue becomes so inwoven with our thoughts and feelings, as to come up spontaneously when our hearts are overflowing. Hence, expressions of tenderness are the last words of their native language which foreigners give up; and in times of excitement, and even delirium, they are sure to come back."[8] Since Jesus used the word in His prayer, it was quite natural for Paul to use the same term for Father, both when he wrote of the Spirit's filial cry in Galatians and of the believer's cry in Romans. The Greek word for Father which follows "Abba" is added to make the expression understandable to those who were not familiar with Aramaic.

The freedom of the sons of God is an inward, voluntary, joyful bondage to Christ, our Saviour and Elder Brother. It is expressed in the words of the Psalmist: "I delight to do thy will, O my God." (Psalm 40:8.) No outward authority could ever produce such filial, trusting love within the heart. Therefore, outward or external authority cannot possibly accomplish the ends of salvation. In the family of God, the children are not under law but under grace, and the requirements of grace are not lighter than those of law but greater and more searching. Now read the closing verses of the eighth chapter of Romans (verses 28-39), and see how the Apostle leads those who have some assurance of sonship up the sunlit summit of salvation.

The question with which this chapter began has not been answered categorically. Perhaps it cannot be. Certainly there is no magical or infallible formula which can be followed in order to attain complete assurance of sonship in God's family. Assurance must come as Christian experience widens and deepens. It comes in a gradual, natural way to those Christians who make diligent use of the means of grace which God has given us. It often comes unexpectedly to those who faithfully perform their daily Christian duty without any thought or hope of gaining by their fidelity an assurance of salvation. It is far, far more important for a Christian to be concerned about his loyalty to Christ and his faithfulness in performing his Christian duties, than about his assurance of salvation.

Chapter 4

GUIDANCE FOR SPIRITUAL PILGRIMS

"Howbeit when he, the Spirit of truth, is come, he will guide you into all truth: for he shall not speak of himself; but whatsoever he shall hear, that shall he speak: and he will shew you things to come." — JOHN 16:13.

ABRAHAM KUYPER, the Dutch Protestant theologian, in his book on the Holy Spirit speaks of the College of the Apostles, of which Jesus was the one Master Teacher. Indeed, it was an incomparable divinity school, or theological seminary, in which the Twelve were instructed for three years as they lived with Jesus and sat at His feet. The "Training of the Twelve," according to A. B. Bruce in his book with that title, was the greatest work that Jesus did while He was on earth, the work which made possible the continuation of His mission after He returned to the bosom of His Father.

Before the separation came, Jesus gathered His disciples about Him for final instructions. He said to them frankly that He had many things to say to them which they were not able to bear at that time. He longed to impart other truths to them which they were as yet incapable of receiving and understanding, so, matchless teacher that He was, He refrained from doing so. It was then that He made them the promise that when the Holy Spirit was come, He would guide them into all truth. And further than that, the Spirit would show them truth in the days ahead which had not at that time come into actuality. This promise was gloriously fulfilled in the lives of the Apostles, as a study of the New Testament abundantly shows. However, it is not enough that the promise was fulfilled in them. It must also be fulfilled in the lives of believers in every age if the cause of Christ is to advance continuously and triumphantly. It is an important work of the Spirit to furnish guidance for spiritual pilgrims when they enter the strange, new world of Christian faith.

GUIDANCE IN A NEW SPIRITUAL COUNTRY

As a man who can see directs one who is blind, as a shepherd guides his flock, as a teacher instructs his pupil, so the Holy Spirit is promised to Christians as their guide in the strange, new spiritual country into which they have entered. His work is not to reveal new truth, for a perfect revelation of God and His gracious purposes of redemption has already been given in the life, work, teaching, and death of Jesus Christ. "He shall not speak of himself; but whatsoever he shall hear, that shall he speak." Rather, He is to be the guide of Christians in an unfamiliar and untraveled land, and their dependable helper (Comforter) amid all the experiences of life.

A guide in a strange country not only shows the way but also points out the beauties and warns of the dangers of the journey. Unusual and unexpected sights are explained to the travelers as they journey along the way. So the Holy Spirit in His work of guidance into all truth makes known to Christians each day of their earthly pilgrimage more and more of the truths of the Gospel, more and more of the saving love and sustaining power of Christ. At the same time, He continually warns of the dangers which beset the path of every pilgrim in the realm of faith.

DANGERS

Let us think first of the dangers present in the new country which the Holy Spirit, as our guide, will point out and warn against. Further than that, as the Comforter of the followers of Christ, He will supply the necessary strength to avoid these dangers, or to overcome them.

Growth in the spiritual life, as every Christian knows, is attended by ups and downs, gains and setbacks, sickness and health, even as in physical life. The very urgency and frequency of the warnings in the New Testament against sin, spiritual dullness, and lack of effort on the part of a Christian indicate an ever-present peril confronting him. "Work out your own salvation with fear and trembling." (Philippians 2:12.) "Give diligence to make your calling and election sure." (II Peter 1:10.) "Resist the devil, and he will flee from you." (James 4:7.) "Let us lay aside every weight, and the sin which doth so easily beset us, and let us run with patience the race that is set before us." (Hebrews 12:1.) These warnings and exhortations — many others might be quoted — clearly indicate that a Christian can never afford to be at ease in Zion and should never serenely fold his hands and wait for something to be done for him by the Lord which he should be doing for himself.

The blessed truth is that the Holy Spirit as He guides spiritual pilgrims puts it into their hearts both to recognize and to hate sin and to struggle daily for growth in grace. At the same time, He gives the spiritual strength necessary to enable them to make progress in the struggle. The Apostle Paul, in the seventh chapter of Romans, sets down a revealing account of his own spiritual pilgrimage. How familiar the words sound to us when we hear him say: "The good that I would I do not: but the evil which I would not, that I do." (Romans 7:19.) His desperation in his contact with evil is expressed in the words of the twenty-fourth verse: "O wretched man that I am! who shall deliver me from the body of this death?" His victory and security are set forth in the two verses immediately following: "I thank God through Jesus Christ our Lord. . . . There is therefore now no condemnation to them which are in Christ Jesus, who walk not after the flesh, but after the Spirit." No condemnation, but instead sufficient spiritual help given to spiritual pilgrims to make it possible for them to overcome the dangers of their journey, and to reach victoriously their destination.

BEAUTIES OF THE NEW COUNTRY

It is not enough for the dangers of the new country to be pointed out to travelers along the way. They need to see the beauties of the journey also, lest they grow tired and discouraged. It is the work of the Holy Spirit, as the guide of Christians, to reveal these beauties which are hidden from the sight of an ordinary man and to clear the vision of the pilgrims so that they can understand and appreciate them. "The natural man receiveth not the things of the Spirit of God: for they are foolishness unto him: neither can he know them, because they are spiritually discerned. But he that is spiritual [guided by the Spirit] judgeth [discerneth] all things." (See I Corinthians 2:14-15.)

Who could see beauty in the trial and death of our Master, or in the cross on which He was crucified and which has become the supreme symbol of Christianity, unless he was taught by the Holy Spirit? The communion of the Lord's Supper, the only memorial Jesus left of His life and work, would never have been perpetuated throughout the centuries unless Christian people had been given spiritual illumination to see its beauty, to understand its significance, and to appropriate its sustaining strength.

Not only does the Spirit open up to Christians the beauty and meaning of the Lord's Supper, but it is He who illuminates their minds as they read and study the Holy Scriptures. "The Spirit of God maketh the reading, but especially the preaching, of the word, an effectual means of convincing and converting sinners, and of building them up in holiness and comfort through faith unto salvation." (Shorter Catechism, Question 89.) The Spirit does not speak of or from Himself. He has no new truth to reveal. Rather, He opens up to the followers of Christ the meaning and beauty of the truth already revealed by our Saviour, a complete and inspired record of which is contained in our Bibles.

Phillips Brooks has a great sermon on the subject, "The Beauty of a Life of Service." In it, he makes this challenging observation:

"It is not your business and mine to study whether we shall get to heaven, even to study whether we shall be good men; it is our business to study how we shall come into the midst of the purposes of God and have the unspeakable privilege in these few years of doing something of His work. . . . You say, 'What can I do?' You can furnish one Christian life."⁹ The beauty of a life of service is spiritually discerned, and the growth in beauty of a Christian's life is the work of the Holy Spirit.

Ever Advancing

As guide in his spiritual pilgrimage, the Spirit leads a Christian ever forward on his journey.

The Old Testament speaks of God's people as strangers and pilgrims on the earth, ever seeking a better land. Of course there is truth in that conception of life, but it seems to fall below the level of truth in the New Testament. The New Testament Christian, guided by the Spirit, believes that "this is my Father's world" and that eternal life begins here and now when a man accepts Christ as his Saviour. It is in this sense that Paul states that our citizenship is even now in heaven. Believers are pilgrims not only on earth but in the Kingdom of Heaven, pilgrims ever expecting greater spiritual blessings, and receiving those blessings as their faith grows strong enough to "possess their possessions."

Forward guidance is not only given to the individual Christian but also to the Church of Christ, the Body of Christ made up of individual Christians. Throughout the Christian world, under the inspiration of the Spirit, there seems to be arising a fresh and enlarged conception of the Church and its place in God's redemptive plans. The Church is the custodian of the sacraments, holy ordinances instituted by Christ. To the Church has been committed the means of grace which are necessary for growth and advancement in the Christian life. Within the Church the Spirit carries on His peculiar or particular work in the heart of a Christian. Through the Church, and by means of the Church, He carries on His work in the world. Martin Luther went so far as to say that no man can have God as his Father who does not have the Church as his Mother. The Holy Spirit leads the Church ever forward, and leads ever forward the Christian within the Church.

> "I love Thy Church, O God:
> Her walls before Thee stand,
> Dear as the apple of Thine eye,
> And graven on Thy hand."[10]

EXALTATION OF CHRIST

As guide in the new spiritual country, a very special work of the Holy Spirit is the exaltation of Christ and His work. "They hated me without a cause," said Jesus. "But when the Comforter is come . . . he shall testify of me." (See John 15:25-26.) When a Christian begins to understand, appreciate, and love Christ more, he has convincing evidence in his heart of the work of the Holy Spirit. Whenever a man finds that he is growing more Christlike in his dealings with his fellow men, in his attitude toward life, in his everyday walk and conversation, he may be very sure that the Holy Spirit is working in him a miracle of grace.

The word intolerance is not a popular word today. However, there is a sense in which it may properly be used of the Holy Spirit. When Christ is not exalted in His Church, or in a Christian's life, the Holy Spirit is grieved, and His fire is quenched. "Wherefore I give you to understand, that no man speaking by the Spirit of God calleth Jesus accursed: and that no man can say that Jesus is the Lord, but by the Holy Ghost." (I Corinthians 12:3.) We often sing the great hymn which begins with the words, "I love to tell the story." Telling the story of Jesus and His love to the hearts of believers so that they may tell it to the world is a work of the Spirit that is carried on as long as life lasts. Whenever we tell this story, however faltering and imperfect may be our words, the evidence of the work of the Spirit in our hearts is clear and should be convincing.

When we read in Scripture that the Holy Spirit fell on certain persons and they began to speak as the Spirit gave them utterance, what was it they said? Not something new, or weird, or unintelligible; rather, they began to tell the old, old story of Jesus and His love. It often happens in our day that people who have been familiar with the Church and with Christianity all their lives begin to see a new meaning in these things, a new meaning for themselves and for the world. They may be surprised to find a new love and loyalty to Christ in their hearts, and a new desire to live, not for themselves, but for Him who died for them, and rose again. When such an experience comes, you can be very sure that the Holy Spirit is at work in your heart.

Things to Come

It is easy to misunderstand the meaning of Jesus when He said: "He [the Spirit] will shew you things to come." It is not the office of the Holy Spirit to unveil the future to a Christian and make him a prophet of coming events. The New Testament prophet was a preacher, a forth-teller of the good news of salvation rather than a fore-teller of the future. Jesus was promising His followers that the Spirit would interpret to them the meaning of events in the future, some of them in the immediate future and others "far down the future's broadening way."

The things in the immediate future which the Master could not make the disciples understand were the Crucifixion, the Resurrection, and the Ascension. He had spoken many times of all three, but even the best of the Apostles were "dull of hearing," and not one of them had a true understanding of what was said. When the door of the tomb closed upon the lifeless body of the blessed Lord, there was doubtless not a person living who believed in his heart that Jesus would rise again. The events themselves had to take place, and then, in the illumination of the Spirit at Pentecost and ever thereafter, believers would be able to "bear" and appropriate their message.

The late Archbishop Temple in his second volume of *Readings in Saint John's Gospel,* lists the following examples of Apostolic teaching concerning themes which, when the Lord was speaking to the disciples, were among the things that were yet to come:

"For he hath made him to be sin for us, who knew no sin; that we might be made the righteousness of God in him." (II Corinthians 5:21.)

"Being justified freely by his grace through the redemption that is in Christ Jesus: whom God hath set forth to be a propitiation through faith in his blood, to declare his righteousness . . ." (Romans 3:24-25.)

"Therefore we are buried with him by baptism into death: that like as Christ was raised up from the dead by the glory of the Father, even so we also should walk in newness of life." (Romans 6:4.)

"But God, who is rich in mercy, for his great love wherewith he loved us, even when we were dead in sins, hath quickened us together with Christ, (by grace ye are saved;) and hath raised us up together, and made us sit together in heavenly places in Christ Jesus." (Ephesians 2:4-6.)

"Having therefore, brethren, boldness to enter into the holiest by the blood of Jesus, by a new and living way, which he hath consecrated for us, through the veil, that is to say, his flesh." (Hebrews 10:19-20.)

After the death, resurrection, and ascension of Jesus had taken place the disciples were bewildered and fearful, but they waited prayerfully in Jerusalem in obedience to the command of their Lord. When the Day of Pentecost was fully come and the Spirit entered into His distinctive ministry on earth, these same timid, fearful disciples were transformed into bold and effective preachers and teachers of the Gospel.

An important and more distant truth included in the things to come concerned the Church, its nature, organization, and work. Jesus spoke very little of the Church as such. Paul and the other New Testament authors spoke and wrote much about the Church. Under the inspiration of the Holy Spirit, they took the truth already revealed in Christ, and when the time came applied it to that institution which carries on the work of the Master on earth. It was under the inspiration of the Spirit that Paul called the Church the Body of Christ, and the Bride of Christ.

Now, we all know that in spite of the work of the Spirit, the Visible Church has made many mistakes, and has within its membership some very imperfect Christians. However, the long history of the Church shows very plainly that it has within itself the principle and power of perpetual renewal, correction, and growth. Whatever others may call that power, members who know their Bibles must call it the Holy Spirit.

> "Crowns and thrones may perish,
> Kingdoms rise and wane,
> But the Church of Jesus
> Constant will remain."[11]

The work of the Spirit in showing and interpreting things when they come is carried on continually in the life and experience of Christians. How else could they be "overcomers" in a world which is so utterly different from the world of Jesus' time, and which presents new problems in each succeeding age? It has been said that an army on the march is not so powerful as an idea whose time has come. A better way for a Christian to express the thought is to say and believe that no force is powerful enough to stand against the Holy Spirit as He interprets to Christians their duty in every present circumstance of life and imparts to them strength and determination to perform that duty.

Because the Spirit has been at work, down through the centuries, in showing things which have come, followers of Jesus in the twentieth century have a far more complete understanding of the meaning of Christianity than did His followers in the first century. Professor A. N. Whitehead of Harvard seems to be among the prophets when he writes: "The progress of humanity can be defined as the process of transforming society so as to make the original Christian ideals increasingly practicable for its individual members."[12] Whenever men find in themselves a keener conscience, a deeper desire to put into practice the teachings of Jesus, and a will to use their influence, power, and money that this may be done, they have in themselves strong evidence of the work of the Holy Spirit in "showing things to come."

Summing up what has been said in this chapter, the three general lines of evidence of the presence and work of the Holy Spirit in the life of a Christian are: (1) Spiritual guidance in life; (2) Increased love and loyalty to Jesus; (3) Recognition of eternal truths heretofore obscure, whose time has come. For my part, I am glad to acknowledge, humbly and gratefully, my complete indebtedness to the Holy Spirit for everything worth while I have ever done, and for all the growth in my Christian life that the years have brought me.

Chapter 5

THE INTERCESSION OF THE SPIRIT

"Likewise the Spirit also helpeth our infirmities: for we know not what we should pray for as we ought: but the Spirit itself maketh intercession for us with groanings which cannot be uttered."

— ROMANS 8:26.

THE REAL MEANING of Paul's words about the intercession of the Holy Spirit is obscure to many Christians. Since the meaning is obscure, the value of the doctrine of the intercession of the Spirit is often neglected if not lost altogether. Understood aright, it can become one of the most comforting and encouraging truths of Scripture.

It is both interesting and instructive to note the uses of the word "groan" in that portion of the eighth chapter of Romans where the Apostle writes of the Spirit's intercession. In verse 22, the whole creation is said to groan and travail in pain. The next verse states that even those who have received the first fruits of the Spirit groan inwardly as they wait for the completion of their adoption into the family of God. The twenty-sixth verse makes the startling statement that the Spirit groans as He makes intercession for believers. We are not surprised at the statement that unredeemed men groan in the bondage of sin. Nor are we disturbed greatly by the assertion that believers groan as they await complete deliverance from sin. But we are amazed to learn that the Holy Spirit, Himself, groans as He makes intercession for the saints.

Paul's climactic use of the word "groan" emphasizes the marred harmony of life in the world as it came from the creative hand of God. Nature may be "red in tooth and claw," as Tennyson says in "In Memoriam," but it was not so originally. Man's inhumanity to man makes countless thousands mourn because sin has changed humanity into inhumanity. The turbid ebb and flow of human misery, of which Matthew Arnold speaks in "Dover Bridge," is the result of the work of sin in the hearts and lives of men who were created in the image of God. What better word could be used than groan to picture the condition of an unredeemed sinner's heart? But why should the Holy Spirit groan?

The Help of the Spirit in Intercession

When Paul spoke of the Spirit helping our infirmity, he used a very meaningful word for "help." It literally means "laying hold along with." There is only one other passage in the New Testament where the word is used. This is in the tenth chapter of Luke where Martha besought the Master that He bid her sister Mary help her in the task of serving — to lend her a helping hand. The Holy Spirit lends a helping hand to the Christian when he prays.

It is significant that the word "infirmities," found in the King James Version with which most Christians are familiar, is really singular in number, and is so rendered in later versions. The Holy Spirit helpeth our infirmity, said Paul, not our infirmities. It is in the particular infirmity of a Christian in the matter of prayer that a believer in Christ receives help from the Spirit. That infirmity is expressed in the words, "We know not what we should pray for as we ought."

Intercession is the ordinary and somewhat technical term which is used for that portion of a prayer in which God's blessings are sought for others. The prayer of Jesus, recorded in the seventeenth chapter of John, is called His Intercessory Prayer because, after praying for Himself, the larger portion of the prayer is for His disciples, and for those who should believe on Him in the years to come. All the great saints of the Church have been notable exponents of intercessory prayer. Intercession, praying for others, is or should be the main content of the prayers of every Christian.

There is an important difference between the intercession which Christ makes in heaven for His people, spoken of in Hebrews 7:25, and the intercession of the Spirit. The intercession of the Risen and Ascended Lord is entirely apart from believers. It is made in heaven while we are here on earth. It is entirely Scriptural and correct to pray to Christ and beseech Him to intercede for us. However, such a prayer would not seem to be necessary since the Scriptures state that He ever liveth to make intercession for His people, and nothing is said about the necessity of asking Him to do so. But it is both unscriptural and incorrect to pray to the Holy Spirit to intercede for us, for His intercessory work is not apart from the believer but within the believer's own heart. The Spirit's intercession is within the Christian and works along with his own spirit in such a way that it is impossible to distinguish the groaning of the Spirit from the groaning of the Christian's spirit. If this point seems to be labored, it is because I believe that a misunderstanding of this particular teaching of Scripture is often the cause of fantastic, if not fanatical, teachings and practices on the part of otherwise very good people.

Moffatt's translation renders the phrase, "groanings which cannot be uttered," as "sighs that are beyond words." The groans which arise within the heart of a Christian as he prays with the help of the Holy Spirit are indeed beyond the power of words to express. Sentiments or feelings which can easily be put into words are often shallow. The groanings of the Spirit as He intercedes for a Christian when he prays are too deep for human words and arouse within him groanings of his own spirit which never come to the surface of verbal expression. We are wrong when we too easily judge the sincerity of a person by the words he speaks or the noise he makes. A catch of breath, a suppressed sigh, a stifled sob, or a furtive tear may mean more in revealing what is within the heart of a man than a showy demonstration of emotion which may not at all be genuine but entirely superficial.

THE CONTENT OF PRAYER

Some very good authorities hold that the intercession of the Holy Spirit is directed toward the manner of prayer and not toward its content or substance. I believe that both the matter and the manner of prayer are within the scope of the Spirit's help, since both are within the scope of a Christian's infirmity.

Though a believer may know that he is a sinner and may long to be delivered from sin, yet he does not and cannot know fully the desperateness of his condition until it is made known to him by the Spirit. He needs constantly to be reminded of what sin is and what sin does. The experiences of life, especially its successes and accomplishments, may dull the sense of sin in a man's life so that he incurs the danger of holding lightly that which he formerly abhorred. The words of Alexander Pope regarding vice are just as true if the word sin is substituted:

> "Vice is a monster of so frightful mien,
> As to be hated needs but to be seen;
> Yet seen too oft, familiar with her face,
> We first endure, then pity, then embrace."[13]

The intercession of the Holy Spirit keeps the sense of sin keen in the heart of a Christian, and makes deliverance from sin a main portion of his prayers as long as he lives.

Further than that, the Spirit awakens and kindles holy desires within the heart. When "a flame of sacred love" is kindled within "these cold hearts of ours," prayer for ourselves and for others rises from the low plane of our natural wants and wishes to the high plane of God's redemptive purposes for the world and those that dwell therein. It is quite natural for a man, even a converted man, to love the things of the earth more than the things of heaven. A candid examination of the content of your prayers and mine ought to be sufficient to prove that this is true. It is the work of the Holy Spirit to change this, gradually perhaps but surely, until we become more honest when we sing: "I know I love Thee better, Lord, than any earthly thing."

Jesus told His disciples that if they should ask (in prayer) anything in His name, after He had left them, He would do it. (See John 14:13-14.) Unfortunately, too many people have interpreted this as meaning that if we conclude our prayer with the words, "For Jesus' sake," they would act as a kind of magic formula in obtaining the answer. The name of Jesus stands for the character, mission, and work of Jesus on earth. Therefore, to ask anything in His name would be to ask those things which are in accordance with His character and which promote His Kingdom and cause. To such a prayer a Christian can always expect an affirmative answer. It is the work of the Holy Spirit to remove this human disability of not knowing "what we should pray for as we ought."

The Manner of Prayer

The manner of prayer is just as important as the matter. The intercession of the Spirit teaches a Christian how he should pray as well as for what he should pray. Too many public prayers seem to be offered for the praise of men rather than for the mercy of God. Such a prayer was that which was once described as "the most eloquent prayer ever delivered before a Boston audience." The mother of a young man who was unexpectedly called on to lead in public prayer complained to me that he was not given enough time to do himself justice!

Many pray in public, and doubtless also in private, as if they were patronizing the Almighty. They give Him a great deal of current information. Take, as an example, the prayer so often heard, "Bless our great country." Now the Lord already knows whether a country is great or not, and calling it great doesn't deceive Him. Perhaps the best of us would be surprised at the small content remaining in the prayers we offer if we subtract from them all the information we offer Him who knoweth all things.

The Holy Spirit purifies the motives of a Christian when he prays. So much prayer seems to be entirely self-centered and selfish. Of course, there is a legitimate self-interest and we are encouraged by the teachings of Jesus to pray about the small as well as the large concerns of our everyday life. However, when our prayers do not go beyond that which concerns ourselves, or the temporal affairs in which we are interested, the main purpose of prayer and the power of prayer in changing things of the earth are neglected and lost. "Not my will, but thine, be done," prayed our Saviour. It is not our will but God's will which should be the controlling motive of a Christian when he prays. Therefore, the motives which lead us to pray should constantly be referred to the Holy Spirit for purifying.

The Spirit, in His work of intercession, shows one who prays the things he may plead before the Throne of Grace, and how to use them. Such pleas as the sacrifice of Christ, the love of God, the glory of salvation, are the vastest that can be used by mortal man, and are never used in vain. Security against the misuse of these pleas is also a work of the Holy Spirit in the heart of a Christian. Such security is sorely needed, for taking the name of the Lord in vain is a widespread sin. Prayer, with the misuse of God's name, attributes, words, and works, "backfires" and becomes profanity or cursing. "The Lord will not hold him guiltless that taketh his name in vain." (Exodus 20:7.)

It is a common experience for a Christian to be confused and bewildered when he begins to pray. Life is complicated, needs are so many, desires are a mixture of good and bad, demands upon time are insistent and loud, relaxation which is essential for earnest prayer is difficult to attain. It is the Holy Spirit who straightens out all these things, clears our minds, strengthens our hearts, directs our wills, ennobles our spirits, and enables us to pray as we ought.

In the Epistle of Jude, the author speaks of praying in the Holy Spirit. Is there any way of telling whether or not we are praying in the Holy Spirit when we kneel in the privacy of our place of prayer, or stand to lead in public prayer? Can we ever

reach the assurance that the Holy Spirit is indeed making intercession for us with groanings which cannot be uttered?

In the great chapter on gifts of the Spirit, the twelfth chapter
of First Corinthians, Paul states that no man can say that Jesus is
the Lord but by the Holy Spirit. If a man confesses Jesus Christ
as his Lord and Master, earnestly tries to serve Him day by day,
and prays with His cause and Kingdom uppermost in his heart,
he can be assured that he is praying in the Spirit. Whatever our
weaknesses may be, however stammering may be our tongues,
and however we may fall short of the glory of God, we can rest
assured that the Holy Spirit is interceding for us with groanings
which cannot be uttered, as long as the earnest desire of our souls
is that Christ shall be Lord of all. "He that searcheth the hearts
knoweth what is the mind of the Spirit, because he maketh
intercession for the saints according to the will of God." (Romans
8:27.)

Chapter 6

SEALED UNTO THE DAY OF REDEMPTION

> "In whom also after that ye believed, ye were sealed with that holy Spirit of promise." — EPHESIANS 1:13.

WHEN THE APOSTLE PAUL used a figure of speech to illustrate and explain a spiritual truth, he always chose one which was familiar to those whom he was instructing. Common custom among them would cause them to understand the figure, usually without the application having to be pointed out. However difficult his figures may appear at this time, we may be very sure that they were not difficult when they were originally used. Thus when Paul spoke of the sealing of the Spirit to people who lived in Ephesus, where an extensive maritime trade was carried on, they knew very well what he was talking about.

THE USE OF SEALS IN THE BIBLE

A seal in Biblical times, as is also true in our day, was an expressive symbol, or sign, to which custom and usage gave a recognized meaning and significance. All civilized peoples and nations have made use of seals. They are used for three general purposes: (1) As a mark of ownership placed by one on property he has purchased; (2) As a stamp of authority on a proclamation, or on an agreement; (3) As a pledge of security, or of sacredness.

The three uses of a seal, listed above, can all be illustrated by incidents drawn from the Scriptures.

Ownership

In the thirty-second chapter of Jeremiah the prophet describes the purchase of a field in Anathoth from Hanameel, his uncle's son. He weighed out to the owner of the field the money, subscribed the evidence, sealed the evidence, and took witnesses. We would say that the prophet signed the deed, had his signature witnessed, placed the legal seal on the instrument of purchase, and paid down the money in full.

It is instructive, as well as comforting, to note the use Paul made of the word seal as a mark of God's ownership. "The foundation of God standeth sure, having this seal, The Lord knoweth them that are his. And, Let every one that nameth the name of Christ depart from iniquity." (II Timothy 2:19.) The seal he describes is the mark, in a Christian's life, of God's ownership of the Christian.

Authority

As a symbol of authority, the seal was used before the art of writing was generally practiced, and took the place of a signature. When placed on a document, it gave that document legal standing. Both signatures and seals are now used on legal instruments. Each state of our nation has its own seal, and the United States makes use of what is known as "The Great Seal."

In the book of Esther (see third chapter) King Ahasuerus of Persia was persuaded by Haman to issue a proclamation for the slaughter of all the Jews living in his kingdom. Haman was entrusted with the writing of the proclamation, but in order to make it authoritative, the king took the signet ring from his hand and gave it to Haman that the decree might bear the royal seal.

When the body of Jesus, after the crucifixion, was laid in the tomb, His enemies were afraid that the disciples would steal Him away and so make it appear that He had risen from the dead. On the authority of Pilate, a stone was placed at the door of the sepulchre, stamped with the Roman seal, and a watch was set.

The seal made it an offense against the Empire to tamper with the stone.

Security

When Daniel was thrown into the den of lions, "a stone was brought, and laid upon the mouth of the den; and the king sealed it with his own signet, and with the signet of his lords; that the purpose might not be changed concerning Daniel." (See Daniel 6:17.) The purpose of the Lord for the final and complete redemption of His people is authenticated and made sure by the Holy Spirit. "Grieve not the holy Spirit of God, whereby ye are sealed unto the day of redemption." (Ephesians 4:30.)

Ownership, Authority, and Security are all expressed in the verse of Scripture with which this chapter begins: "In whom also after that ye believed, ye were sealed with that holy Spirit of promise." (Ephesians 1:13.) The Gentile Christians of Ephesus, by the kindness and mercy of God, had been received into the Church and made partakers of the benefits of redemption on the same terms as the Jews — faith in Christ. The Holy Spirit was given them as a seal, said Paul, becoming the evidence of God's ownership, the divine authority authenticating their salvation, and the security with which they could now receive and exercise the heavenly grace bestowed upon them.

THE SEAL OF OWNERSHIP

The first and, it seems to me, the main idea in Paul's use of the metaphor of sealing with reference to the Holy Spirit is that of divine ownership of those to whom the Spirit was given.

In ancient times, and doubtless when Paul visited Ephesus, an extensive trade in timber was carried on. It was customary for a shipmaster, or some agent of a distant purchaser, to examine the timber offered for sale, select the pieces he wished to buy, and then stamp the selected pieces in such a way that his ownership would be known, and could be later proved. When the time came for removing the purchased timber, another agent of the owner would appear with a signet corresponding to the stamp and

take possession of all timber which he found stamped according
to the seal.

A similar method in the purchase of timber has been used in
our own land. In the writer's own family a very good illustration
is available. For many years, a brother was an agent for a firm of
railroad crosstie contractors. The method of purchase was for the
agent to go through timbered land where crossties were being
hewn out by hand. The ties selected for purchase would be
marked with an iron instrument, a process called "spotting."
Later, the ties purchased and spotted would be collected and
assembled for shipment.

Perhaps during Paul's long stay in Ephesus, he often watched
the shipmasters as they selected and stamped, or sealed, pieces of
timber. The thought must have come to him that in some similar
way God chooses and seals those who accept Christ. The instrument of sealing was the Holy Spirit, who imprints the image of
Christ upon the soul of the believer. This imprint was the mark
of God's ownership. "Know ye not that your body is the temple
of the Holy Ghost which is in you, which ye have of God, and
ye are not your own? For ye are bought with a price." (I Corinthians 6:19-20.) When the Lord looks upon a believer, He sees
the imprint of the seal rather than the faults and shortcomings of
the one bearing the imprint. "The Lord knoweth them that
are his."

A writer on the ritual worship of the ancient Jews states that it
was the custom of the high priest to select the lambs for sacrifice
in the Temple, and to inspect them with care. If the lamb was
found to be without blemish or defect, the high priest would
stamp it with the seal of the Temple. The lamb was thus certified
as fit for sacrifice and was reserved for that purpose. With this
custom in mind, think of the Lamb of God presenting Himself
for inspection and selection at the River Jordan. Under His
Father's inspection, He was found to be without spot or blemish.
This fact was proclaimed from heaven by a voice saying: "This
is my beloved Son, in whom I am well pleased." (Matthew 3:
17.) The Holy Spirit then descended as a dove and sat upon

Him, giving Him the seal of God's ownership, authority, and security.

The selecting and sealing of lambs for Temple sacrifice is not a complete illustration of the sealing of believers, in that the lambs had no choice in the matter. God does not — cannot — place His seal of ownership upon a man until that man voluntarily surrenders himself to God. If, under pressure of the things of the world or the attractiveness of things sinful, a man who claims to have accepted Christ as his Saviour does not make a complete dedication of himself to God, how can he be sealed? Surely the Lord will not place His seal of ownership upon that which does not belong entirely to Him. Even from a human standpoint, such an act would not be honorable. John tells us (see John 2: 23-24) that when Jesus was in Jerusalem at the Passover Feast many believed in His name when they saw the miracles which He did; but Jesus did not trust Himself to them. The great and essential question for a believer who longs for the sealing of the Spirit is here plainly set forth: Can Jesus trust Himself to me? Can He give me the signet ring of the Spirit for signing my prayers and certifying my service without compromising Himself?

A warning may very well be sounded here for those not fully instructed in the things of the Kingdom. The sealing of the Spirit does not give a believer great and extraordinary power, except in the sense that real spirituality is extraordinary in a world of secularism. When a follower of Jesus is sealed, or stamped with His image, he receives the spirit of humility, love, unselfishness, and sacrifice. Such Christlike qualities of character as these, when found in a Christian, are authentic evidence that he has been sealed.

THE SEAL OF AUTHORITY

The divine authority of the seal brings validity and stability to a dedicated Christian life and, at the same time, strength and sturdiness to the faith and service of the one sealed. Since spiritual impressions made upon the soul of man are apt to be frail and fleeting, it is vastly important that they be fixed and made permanent. One day we may feel that our lives have been

definitely touched and changed by the Lord. The next day, to
our dismay, the feeling may be entirely gone. With the departure
of this feeling, we become discouraged and are in danger of
returning to the fleshpots of Egypt.

> "Prone to wander, Lord, I feel it,
> Prone to leave the God I love;
> Here's my heart, O take and seal it,
> Seal it for Thy courts above."[14]

The sealing of the Spirit gives validity to faith, stability to
worship, and effectiveness to service.

A Christian's desire for spiritual things is sealed by the Spirit.
At the beginning of his Christian experience he may feel a great
enthusiasm for Christ and His cause. This enthusiasm ought to
grow deeper in his life, day by day, but often it does not. And
it never grows without molestation from the enemy of all spiritual
things. All the agencies of the Devil are set to work to extinguish
the sacred flame of spiritual life. The adversary never permits a
follower of Jesus to rest in peace and at ease in this world. Dr.
C. R. Vaughan has an unusually beautiful passage expressing
this thought. The desire for eternal life, he says, "is not like the
love-light of the Hindoo maiden set afloat as the dusk settles down
on the smooth waters of the sacred Ganges and under the still air
of an Indian summer evening. It is a point of slender flame, no
bigger than the blaze of a candle, set afloat on the wild waves of
the tempest-ridden seas. The mad waters are lashing at it; the
winds are blowing a hurricane upon it; it is amazing that it lives
for a moment. But, strange to see and strange to say, clear, shin-
ing through the darkness and the storm; now riding on the crest
of the billows; now buried in the belly of the deep, that slender
flame floats unharmed. It has been sealed by the Holy Ghost,
and in that impervious casing of covenanted grace it will ride
out the tempest, safe and inextinguishable."[15]

A Christian's hatred of sin and evil is sealed by the Holy Spirit.
He is not snatched away from temptation and conflict to be safe
in some Beulah Land while others are perishing. Rather, he is
made secure in the possession of divine grace as he struggles in

his life against the forces of evil surrounding him. If a man is sincerely to hate sin, he must face it, see it at work, and come to know that its wages are death. Our Saviour, while on earth, was daily in contact with sin, and with sinners. Indeed, He could not have redeemed men from sin without having intimately known sin. He smelled its hot and fetid breath. He felt its terrible tentacles trying to crush the lifeblood from His heart. He knew sin, what it was and what it did, and hated it with a divine hatred. Let it be said, however, that He never hated a sinner. To be a follower of Jesus, a man must be sealed by the Spirit in an everlasting hatred of sin. If and when a professing Christian finds that he does not hate sin as he should, but tolerates it, or compromises with it, he can well doubt whether he has ever been sealed by the Spirit.

A Christian's appreciation of the great truths of salvation and a growing understanding of these truths are sealed by the Spirit. The preaching of the Cross is foolishness to those who are lost, but to those who are saved, and sealed, it is the power of God and the wisdom of God. The resources of God, symbolized by the Cross, are sufficient for every need. He who saves us and places the seal of His ownership and authority upon us is able and willing to help us in all our difficulties, and to make us more than conquerors amid all the experiences of life.

> "Salvation! O the joyful sound;
> 'Tis pleasure to our ears;
> A sovereign balm for every wound,
> A cordial for our fears."[16]

A Christian's grasp of the great and precious promises of the Bible and his capacity to claim them for himself come to him as a result of the sealing of the Holy Spirit. In trials of faith, when the providences of God seem to deny His love, how precious the promises become! It is often found that they are being fulfilled at the very time they seem to be denied. The sealing of the Spirit makes the promises, which are sometimes like checks written in invisible ink, open up to a Christian, along the journey of life, in all their wealth and fullness.

A Christian is sealed for the service of God by the Holy Spirit. The authority of God claims him, and the grace of God sustains him as he goes in and out, doing his Master's will. When Jesus was sealed by the Spirit at the River Jordan, He began His ministry of preaching, teaching, and healing. "God anointed Jesus of Nazareth with the Holy Ghost and with power: who went about doing good, and healing all that were oppressed of the devil; for God was with him." (Acts 10:38.) The sealing of the Spirit furnishes a Christian with perseverance and strength, wisdom and guidance, in the service of his Master. How else could the Church have continued to live and grow down through the ages in the face of so many enemies and in spite of so many unworthy members if the redeemed had not been sealed for service? How could it, otherwise, remain steadfast today under such suffering as it has endured in Europe and Asia, and such prosperity as has been its lot in America? Surely the daily prayer of all true Christians should be: "Seal us for service, today."

The third general work effected by the Holy Spirit in His sealing ministry, the security of the believer, will be set forth in the succeeding chapter.

Under the Old Testament dispensation, the men of Israel received as a seal of the ownership and authority of God the physical rite of circumcision. Like irrational animals they were thus marked. Under the New Testament dispensation, believers in Christ are sealed as sons of God by the Holy Spirit. The stamp of God is placed on their souls, rather than on their bodies. This stamp, or seal, is a guarantee of all God's covenanted promises, all the heavenly blessings He has prepared for those who love and serve Him. Jesus said that the Father gives the Holy Spirit to them that ask Him. In giving the Holy Spirit to His children, God gives Himself. What more could a Christian ask? What more could he expect, or even imagine?

"Eye hath not seen, nor ear heard, neither have entered into the heart of man, the things which God hath prepared for them that love him. But God hath revealed them unto us by his Spirit." (See I Corinthians 2:9-10.)

Chapter 7

FORETASTE OF GLORY DIVINE

"That holy Spirit of promise . . . is the earnest of our inheritance
until the redemption of the purchased possession."

— EPHESIANS 1:13-14.

WHEN CHRISTIANS ARE SEALED by the Holy Spirit, this gift
of the Holy Spirit to dwell henceforth in their lives is an "earnest"
of the inheritance which they shall one day receive in all its fullness. The word used by Paul for "earnest," like the word used
for "seal," was a mercantile term familiar to the people. It de-
noted an advance gift or token payment given as assurance of
the fulfillment of a bargain, or promise, and was similar in quality
to the benefit later to be bestowed. If wages were the question,
a part was advanced. We would call this the payment of a re-
tainer. If land was being sold, a clod of earth was given. This
use of an "earnest," formerly quite common, has been superseded
by a written contract.

The word "earnest," therefore, does not signify merely a pledge
deposited for a time and ultimately to be reclaimed, but rather
an installment paid immediately as a proof of good faith. It was
an actual portion of the whole which was later to be paid in full.
When the Apostle Paul spoke of the gift of the Holy Spirit as an

earnest, he must have meant that this brought believers a fore-taste of future blessedness and a pledge, or guarantee, that the whole would be given in due time.

The Feast of Pentecost was one of the three great annual celebrations among the Jews. It was held at the beginning of the harvest time and all the people assembled in Jerusalem for the celebration. On the appointed day, a delegation of priests from the Temple would go to the nearest harvest field, followed by the people, and cut a few sheaves of grain. These sheaves were brought into the Temple, amid loud demonstrations of joy, and offered to the Lord. They were the earnest of the harvest, a pledge of bread once again given to Israel.

It was on the Day of Pentecost that the Holy Spirit was poured out from heaven upon men. Paul, fully understanding the significance of this, explained that the gift of the Spirit was the earnest of a Christian's inheritance until the redemption of the purchased possession.

The Foretaste

As an earnest, the Holy Spirit is a foretaste of the blessings God has prepared for His people. Whatever we may think of heaven, we must square our thoughts with the foretaste already given.

> "Blessed assurance, Jesus is mine!
> O what a foretaste of glory divine!"

Continuity of Spiritual Blessings

The earnest being an actual part of that which later was to be paid or given in full, it follows that the spiritual blessings of heaven will possess a continuity with the blessings brought a believer in this life by the gift of the Spirit. In spite of the teachings of Scripture, men are prone to think of the life after death as entirely different from the present life. They hope that, though they lie down as sinners, they shall rise up as saints. Some seem to believe that they can die loving material things on earth and awaken loving spiritual things in heaven, or die without having rendered any real service to the Lord and awaken with a consuming zeal to serve Him. Such hopes are vain.

The teaching of Jesus was that spiritual life — life with an eternal quality — begins here and now. "This *is* eternal life, that they know thee the only true God, and Jesus Christ whom thou hast sent."[17] Condemnation also begins in this life. "He that believeth not is condemned already, because he hath not believed in the name of the only begotten Son of God." (John 3:18.) Life does not break off at death and become separated from all that has gone before. Life *continues* after death, the same in kind though different in degree.

> "No, no! the energy of life may be
> Kept on after the grave, but not begun;
> And he who flagged not in the earthly strife,
> From strength to strength advancing — only he,
> His soul well-knit, and all his battles won,
> Mounts, and that hardly, to eternal life."[18]

Identity of Spiritual Blessings

The figure of the earnest teaches not only the continuity but also the identity of blessings here and hereafter. As the token payment is spiritual, so the full possession will be spiritual. "Now this I say, brethren, that flesh and blood cannot inherit the kingdom of God; neither doth corruption inherit incorruption." (I Corinthians 15:50.) Those who know nothing of spiritual things on earth cannot know them in a realm beyond the earth. Dr. Alexander Maclaren said in one of his sermons: "There is no reason to believe that anything in death or beyond it will so alter the set and direction of a man's soul as that it will lead him into a possession of God, and being possessed by Him, which he has not here."

The rich young ruler, with all his attractive personality (Jesus, looking upon him, loved him), could not become a follower of Christ because he was unwilling to surrender himself and be possessed by the Master. Desiring to hold on to the joys of earth, he lost the joys of heaven. Dante relates that in his journey through hell, he saw this young man who "with ignoble spirit, made the great refusal."

The identity of spiritual blessings here and hereafter is not a hard or arbitrary doctrine. When understood aright it is gloriously comforting to suffering saints in their spiritual pilgrimage on earth.

Incompleteness of Present Blessing

Those who are truly Christian possess the Spirit in their lives, but not all the Spirit. They have God as their Father, and He has them as His children, yet common experience shows that the circle is not yet complete but has some awful gaps in it. Because of man's sin and willfulness, God who gave the Spirit without measure to His Son cannot do so with us. This incompleteness can and should be lessened day by day as Christians place themselves consciously under the influence of the means of grace ordained for spiritual growth and rid themselves of that which grieves or quenches the Spirit.

There is, however, a final completeness that can never be ours in this present life. We have the earnest but will not have the complete inheritance until the redemption of the purchased possession. "Beloved! now are we the sons of God, and it doth not yet appear what we shall be: but we know that, when he shall appear, we shall be like him; for we shall see him as he is." (I John 3:2.)

The Earnest as a Pledge

The earnest of the Spirit is not only a foretaste of glory divine but also a pledge from God that the final possession will be bestowed in due time, and a guarantee that all needed encouragement, guidance, and strength will be supplied until we come to that blessed day.

Immortality

Without an assurance of immortality, all promises of future blessings would be mockery. So far as the record of the Gospels goes, Jesus never concerned Himself about establishing a proof of the immortality of the soul. The people to whom He ministered already believed in immortality, and He took this well-rooted belief and went on from there to teach the blessedness of present and future life in fellowship with Him. "In my Father's house are many mansions . . . I go to prepare a place for you . . . that where I am, there ye may be also." (See John 14:2-3.) "Yet a little while, and the world seeth me no more; but ye see me: because I live, ye shall live also." (John 14:19.)

Perhaps not many of the readers of this book need any proof or guarantee of immortality. It is an article of faith which has dwelt in their hearts from their earliest memory. Yet everyone needs and welcomes a strengthening of that faith. Such refreshment should come to us with every motion of the Spirit within our hearts, every impulse to sacrificial service we feel, every trial we are able to endure with patience, and every sorrow borne with Christian fortitude. These spiritual powers, whose very existence may be unsuspected until the need for them appears, are an earnest of the Holy Spirit and point to the ultimate goal beyond our present sight, giving us strong hope that we shall finally reach that goal in "Canaan's fair and happy land where my possessions lie."

Grace Sufficient

Grace sufficient for the hardship and trials of life is pledged to every Christian when he is given the earnest of the Spirit. He may not be freed from every doubt, for very few ever pass through life without encountering doubts of one kind or another. Honest doubts are healthful when they drive the doubter to seek more earnestly for the truth. "If any man willeth to do his will, he shall know . . ." (John 7:17, A.S.V.) It is the Spirit who makes a man willing to do God's will, and in the doing of His will, doubts dissolve away and trusting faith replaces them.

When a man is confident that he possesses the strength and resources to win the victory, he is much more certain to persevere in his struggles than if he were doubtful of the outcome. This grace sufficient is guaranteed by the earnest. Let us therefore run with patience the race that is set before us.

God's Promise and Oath

The writer of Hebrews uses strong language in proclaiming the integrity of God in the salvation of His people. He states that God, wishing to show more abundantly unto the heirs of promise the immutability of His counsel, confirmed it by an oath, so that by two immutable things — His promise and His oath — in which it was impossible for God to lie, we might have a strong consolation, who have fled for refuge to lay hold upon the hope set before us. (See Hebrews 6:17-18.)

The earnest of the Spirit is God's pledge and oath that He will see us through to the end. The resources of heaven are at the disposal of a Christian who has been sealed. "I am persuaded," wrote Paul — and we may have the same assurance — "that neither death, nor life, nor angels, nor principalities, nor powers, nor things present, nor things to come, nor height, nor depth, nor any other creature, shall be able to separate us from the love of God, which is in Christ Jesus our Lord." (Romans 8:38-39.)

THE COMPLETE INHERITANCE

In the King James Version of the New Testament, the Holy Spirit is said to be the earnest of our inheritance *until* the redemption of the purchased possession. (Ephesians 1:14.) The American Standard Version changes the word "until" to "unto," making the meaning not merely future but purposeful. The Spirit works in our hearts to make us ready and prepared for the full inheritance when the time shall come for us to receive it.

What shall be the nature and the fullness of the complete inheritance of a Christian in the life after death? In their speculation about the future life, men have unfortunately elevated into places of great importance things which are relatively of small importance. In attempting to conceive of a condition be-yond his experience, a man naturally uses the means of negation and of symbolism. These two means of picturing heaven are employed in the Bible and are entirely misunderstood when taken literally. By way of negation, we are told that there shall be no night there, no sea, no curse, no sorrow, and no pain. Positive symbols used are those of golden streets, white robes, crowns, and harps. Both the negative and the positive symbols are used to describe a future state of spiritual blessedness in terms readily understood, even by those who have only a small amount of spiritual insight and intuition.

Since the Holy Spirit is the earnest, and the Holy Spirit is the Third Person of the Trinity, the conclusion must be made that the full inheritance of the saints in light is nothing less than God, Himself. Heaven is to possess God, and to be possessed by Him. This is the highest conception of the future life. "The Lord is the portion of mine inheritance and of my cup." (Psalm 16:5.) We shall be like Him when we see Him as He is.

It must not be concluded from what has been said that heaven will be a place of passivity, or of anything approaching monotony. Rather it shall be a place where, under ideal conditions, those who have received the final inheritance shall continually grow and serve. Paul Hamilton Hayne, the Southern poet, has a beautiful little poem entitled "The True Heaven." Because the poem is not very well known, and because it expressly sets forth the thought I have been trying to present, it is here printed in full:

> "The bliss for which our spirits pine,
>   That bliss we feel shall yet be given,
> Somehow, in some far realm divine,
>   Some marvellous state we call a heaven,
>
> "Is not the bliss of languorous hours,
>   A glory of calm, measured range,
> But life which feeds our noblest powers
>   On wonders of eternal change.
>
> "A heaven of action, freed from strife,
>   With ampler ether for the scope
> Of an immeasurable life
>   And an unbaffled, boundless hope.

"A heaven wherein all discords cease,
    Self-torment, doubt, distress, turmoil,
The care of whose majestic peace
    Is godlike power of endless toil.

"Toil, without tumult, strain or jar,
    With grandest reach of range endued,
Unchecked by even the farthest star
    That trembles through infinitude;

"In which to soar to higher heights
    Through widening ethers stretched abroad,
Till in our onward, upward flights
    We touch at last the feet of God.

"Time swallowed in eternity!
    No future evermore; no past,
But one unending NOW, to be
    A boundless circle round us cast!"[19]

It must be stated, before this chapter ends, with sadness but in all sincerity, that heaven with its full and complete inheritance is not for everyone whom God has created. The Lord longs to have each of us for His own in this life as He longs to have all for His own in the life to come, but it shall be no more true there than it is here. Preparation for the complete possession must be begun and continued here as long as life lasts, else we can have no valid claim on the final inheritance. " 'Believe on the Lord Jesus Christ' if thou wouldst have the earnest, whilst thou dost tabernacle in tents in the wilderness of Time, and if thou wouldst have the inheritance when thou crossest the flood into the goodly land."[20]

Chapter 8

THE LORD'S ANOINTED

"Now he which stablisheth us with you in Christ, and hath anointed us, is God." — II CORINTHIANS 1:21.

THROUGHOUT THE HOLY SCRIPTURES, anointing is the symbol of the bestowal of special divine influence and power. One who was anointed was chosen for a special work and, at the same time, was the recipient of grace sufficient for that work.

In the Old Testament, the priests were anointed before they entered upon the duties of their office. The beautiful 133rd Psalm compares unity of the brethren to the treasured incident in Israel's history when Aaron was anointed high priest: "It is like the precious ointment upon the head, that ran down upon the beard, even Aaron's beard: that went down to the skirts of his garments." (Psalm 133:2.) Kings also were anointed to office, usually by a prophet of the Lord. It was a turning point in the history of Israel when Saul was anointed to be the first king by the prophet Samuel. Later, David was anointed by the same prophet to be king in Saul's stead. Solomon was anointed king by Zadok; Jehu by a young prophet at the direction of Elisha; Joash by Jehoiada.

Peter, in Acts 10:38, speaks of God anointing Jesus of Nazareth with the Holy Spirit and with power. He then adds that Jesus went about doing good, and healing all that were oppressed of the devil; for God was with Him. The word "Messiah" in the Old Testament and the word "Christ" in the New Testament literally mean "The Anointed." Jesus Christ is Jesus, the Anointed of God. When Paul, in the verse at the head of this chapter, speaks of Christians being established (made firm and secure) in Christ the Anointed by being anointed of God, he is stating something far more significant than at first appears. Indeed, he seems to be saying that a Christian is in a very real sense a Christ, chosen, anointed, and sent forth for a particular purpose by God. This is a humbling thought, and also a soul-inspiring one. No Christian would even think of claiming such a high place. Indeed, no Christian can make such a claim, and if he did it would be evidence that he was not a Christian at all. It is the anointing of the Holy Spirit that makes us what God wants us to be — Messiahs, Christs — not in the sense that Jesus is Mediator and Saviour, but men chosen and redeemed, consecrated and sent forth to do the Master's will.

The anointing of the Spirit should not be identified or confused with the regenerating work of the Spirit. Anointing is a special gift for a special purpose to a man who has already been born again. Nor is this gift the same as daily growth in grace and in the knowledge of the Lord, which is known as Sanctification. Rather it is the bestowal of special renewing and refreshing power, ordinarily given for a particular task or an unusual experience. The familiar prayer for an outpouring of the Spirit, which is so frequently made, is really unscriptural. The Holy Spirit was poured out in all His fullness and power on the Day of Pentecost and has not been withdrawn or diminished in power since that day on which He entered into His distinctive ministry in God's redemptive plan. It is Scriptural, however, and necessary for a Christian who would be and do his best to pray for a fresh anointing of the Spirit, and that continually.

Spiritual Sight and Insight

Doubtless there are none who possess perfect physical sight and certainly there are none who possess perfect spiritual sight. Anointing the eyes of a man who is blind does not bestow upon him sight. (The act of Jesus described in John 9:6 as "anointing," when He gave sight to one born blind, was that of rubbing the clay He had made on the blind eyes. This is brought out in the a.s.v. margin.) On the other hand, anointing the eyes of one who can see but whose eyes are weak or irritated brings refreshment and clearer vision. In the spiritual realm, the new birth is accompanied by a new ability to see spiritually. But, like our physical eyes, our spiritual eyes often become tired or irritated, and scarcely able to function. The anointing of the Spirit increases spiritual vision when it is weak, or restores it when it seems to be lost.

Physical blindness is considered one of the greatest afflictions a person may be called upon to bear in his life. Those who possess good vision seldom value their sight as they should. It is when the ability to see begins to fail, and when sight is entirely lost, that a man really appreciates the blessing that has been his. Even more grievous than physical blindness is spiritual blindness. Sadly enough there are far more spiritually blind people in the world than physically blind, and many of them do not sense their condition and are, therefore, unconcerned about it.

A small child was asked what he would wish for most if he should go blind. His reply was: "A little dog to lead me." So it is that Christians in a childish way often ask for blind guidance in their lives rather than for spiritual sight which they need so much and which can be theirs through a fresh anointing of the Spirit.

"Ye have an anointing from the Holy One, and ye know all things," John wrote to his "little children" who were weary and distressed in their contacts with the sinful world. (See I John 2: 20, a.s.v.) "Why is it," asked an unusually sweet-spirited Christian teacher, "that I can't make others see the truth that is dazzling my

eyes?" Many earnest teachers of Christian truth have asked that
question silently in their hearts if not audibly with their lips. The
answer is that spiritual things are spiritually discerned and the
eyes of a man must not only be spiritually opened but spiritually
alert before he can see and understand eternal truth. "The
natural man receiveth not the things of the Spirit of God: for
they are foolishness unto him: neither can he know them, because they are spiritually discerned." (I Corinthians 2:14.)

So it is that when a Christian reads and studies his Bible, when
he prepares to teach a Sunday school lesson or make a talk on a
religious theme, he should pray for an anointing of the Spirit
that he may see and understand the truth himself before he tries
to teach others. It follows then that there should also be a prayer
for an anointing of the eyes of those to be taught, that they may
be led to see and appropriate the truth presented.

> "Silently now I wait for Thee,
> Ready, my God, Thy will to see;
> Open my eyes, illumine me,
> Spirit divine!"[21]

REFRESHMENT AND HEALING

The anointing of the body with oil, or with oil mixed with
perfume, as practiced in Bible times, was for the purpose of
refreshment and of healing. The climate of Palestine was dry
and the heat oppressive. Anointing the head or the body with
fragrant, cooling oil was highly appreciated and everywhere practiced. We remember that Jesus charged His host Simon with
discourtesy because no water had been provided for His feet and
no oil for His head when He entered Simon's home as a guest.

In the Epistle of James (see chapter 5) the elders of the church
were instructed to anoint the sick with oil, in the name of the
Lord, and then to pray for their recovery. This anointing with
oil was not a magic formula, as some have seemed to think.
Rather, it was a symbol of divine blessing, a sacrament, and at the
same time a sensible use of a well-known medical means of pro-
viding soothing refreshment for sick and feverish bodies.

In the heat and conflict of life, Christians often become weary and exhausted. Even the best of them are prone to grow tired and discouraged, and may even wonder at times, "What's the use of it all?" What they need, and what they can have if they possess faith enough to receive it, is a fresh anointing of the Spirit. In the beloved Twenty-third Psalm, David sings, "He restoreth my soul." The meaning is that God revived life within him when it was at a low ebb. Later in the Psalm come the familiar words about anointing: "Thou anointest my head with oil; my cup runneth over."

Of all the dangers Christians encounter in their life and service, the most insidious is that of staleness and lifeless routine. Charles M. Schwab, the steel magnate, is quoted as having said that he feared monotony and boredom in the work of his employees more than any other thing — more than labor disputes and strikes, or any collective difficulty. Many churches and many individual Christians know what it is to be afflicted with such a spiritual disease. One of the charges made against the church at Ephesus, in the second chapter of Revelation, by the Risen Lord, was that they had "left their first love." The members had lost their early enthusiasm, and their spiritual ardor and zeal had flagged. The anointing of the Spirit is the divine means of banishing staleness and boredom in the Christian life and restoring a lost enthusiasm for the Church and for the Kingdom of God.

THE BEAUTY OF HOLINESS

> "God, who touchest earth with beauty,
> Make me lovely, too."

That is what an anointing of the Spirit does for a Christian. When one is refreshed and healed, he becomes more lovely in person and in spirit. The many cosmetics used by women, and sometimes by men, are an almost pathetic indication of the search for beauty. There is a better and surer way to beauty than the way of cosmetics. In Biblical times, anointing with oil was only incidentally for beauty. Primarily the use was for cleansing, soothing, and relaxation, with beauty as a by-product.

Perhaps few of us think as much as we should about being beautiful and attractive Christians. One of the startling differences between Jesus and His Apostles, which any close reader of the Gospels can note, is that His spirit in service was always beautiful while that of His Apostles was often unattractive or repelling. A man of fine Christian character left the room where he had been conferring with fellow Christians. After he had closed the door, one of those remaining was heard to say, "There goes a Christian gentleman!" He then added: "It doesn't hurt any Christian to be a gentleman." It doesn't hurt, but how much it does help!

Those who are outside the Christian family are, too often, not attracted but repelled by what they see in the characters and lives of the Christians with whom they associate. Many have been kept out of church membership by the lack of beauty, if not the outright ugliness, of the dispositions and characters of those who are members. And young men have been turned away from the ministry, when they were seriously considering entering that form of Christian service, by an unlovely spirit in those whom they had a right to expect to find serving the Lord in the beauty of holiness.

On the other hand, there is nothing more comely and nothing which better commends the Gospel to others than a beautiful Christian character. Is it not so with those who are full of years? "The hoary head is a crown of glory, if it be found in the way of righteousness." (Proverbs 16:31.) A calm, tranquil spirit, a fine faith, and a great love — what is more beautiful toward the end of life? Surely, it is also true of those who are young. A young life devoted to great ideals, to unselfishness, to sacrifice, to Christ — a life loyal and faithful and true — what sermon can equal it in drawing men to the foot of the Cross? And so it is with every age of life. It is the mission of the Spirit in His anointing work to bestow this beauty and attractiveness upon a Christian. Surely we should all feel like praying in the spirit of Peter when Jesus was washing his feet: "Not my feet only, Lord, but anoint my head, my hands, my whole body!"

An anointed Christian is not only a beautiful Christian, but a happy Christian. "Man's chief end is to glorify God, and to *enjoy* Him forever," the Shorter Catechism reminds us. David sang in Psalm Forty, the eighth verse: "I delight to do thy will, O my God." Every Christian needs daily an anointing of the Spirit for beauty and for happiness in a world where sin continually works to destroy both.

From Refreshment to Labor

Perhaps there is no word in Christian nomenclature which needs redefining more than the word spiritual. We frequently hear the words "spiritual," "spiritually minded," and "spirit-filled" used to describe a Christian, without very much consistency in the usage. A spiritual man is a man who has been anointed by the Spirit of God and is, as a result, spiritually alert and discerning, radiant and beautiful in his life, and happy in the performance of his Christian duty. People who are emotional in their religion are not necessarily spiritual, nor are those who are able to pray or speak in public. Paul condemned the emotionalism of the Corinthians, and Jesus rebuked the Pharisees who were always eager to pray in public places.

It is instructive to note that Jesus never used the word spiritual. He continually spoke of life that was abundant, submitted to God, directed by purpose, and fulfilling its mission. Paul did use the word spiritual, but when his hearers misunderstood what he was saying, he wrote: "If any man think himself to be a prophet, or spiritual, let him acknowledge that the things that I write unto you are the commandments of the Lord." (I Corinthians 14:37.)

In the Old Testament the word spiritual occurs only once — Hosea 9:7 — where the context shows that it has an entirely different meaning from New Testament usages of the word. However, there are many places where it is stated that the Spirit of God came upon a man, and in each case it was to fit him for a particular work he was to do. For example, Bezaleel was filled with the Spirit of God in wisdom, understanding, knowledge, and all manner of workmanship in order that he might devise cunning works — work in gold, silver, and brass, in the cutting of stones, and in the carving of timber — all for the construction of the Tabernacle and the furnishings. (Exodus 31:3-5.) In Judges the Spirit of God came upon Gideon, Jephthah, and Samson, and in each case it was for the purpose of fitting them for a particular work that needed to be done at the time. The Spirit of God came upon Saul, the king, when he went to the rescue of Jabesh-Gilead; upon David when he was anointed king of Israel; upon Azariah when he went out to meet Asa and persuaded him to put away idolatry.

In Isaiah, eleventh chapter, a great Messianic passage, the prophecy is made that the Spirit of God shall rest upon the Coming One, giving Him wisdom, understanding, counsel, might, knowledge, and the fear of the Lord. A later Messianic prophecy, contained in the sixty-first chapter, speaks of the Spirit of the Lord as anointing the Messiah for His ministry of teaching, preaching, and healing. It was this latter passage that Jesus read and applied to Himself on that memorable day when He preached in the synagogue of His home town, Nazareth: "The Spirit of the Lord is upon me, because he hath anointed me to preach the gospel to the poor; he hath sent me to heal the broken-hearted, to preach deliverance to the captives, and recovering of sight to the blind, to set at liberty them that are bruised, to preach the acceptable year of the Lord." (Luke 4:18-19.)

A Christian, anointed of the Lord, goes in the refreshment he has received to the labor for which he has been chosen. Whether it be a work to be done in the Church, a wrong to be righted in the world, a battle to be fought for truth and righteousness, he goes willingly, gladly, and "if any man draw back, my soul shall have no pleasure in him." (See Hebrews 10:38.) Such a one may truly be called "spiritual." He is the Lord's anointed.

Chapter 9

THE UNITY OF THE SPIRIT
AND THE SPIRIT OF UNITY

"I have declared to you the Divine purpose, and the calling whereby you have been called to take your place in it. I have prayed that you may know its uttermost meaning for yourselves. Prisoner as I am, I can do no more. But I plead with you that you will respond to your calling. Make your conduct worthy of your position. First and foremost, cultivate the meek and lowly mind, the patient forbearance, the charity, without which a common life is impossible. For you must eagerly preserve your spiritual oneness. Oneness is characteristic of the Gospel. Consider its present working and its predestined issue: there is one Body, animated by one Spirit, cherishing one Hope. Look back to its immediate origin: there is one Lord, to whom we are united by one Faith in Him, by one Baptism in His name. Rise to its ultimate source: there is one God, the Father of all, who is over all, through all, and in all." — EPHESIANS 4:1-6. (Paraphrase by J. ARMITAGE ROBINSON.[22])

THE LIFE AND DEATH OF JESUS are historical incidents in this world of space and time. For Christians, this means that the incarnation of God in human form, and the death of God's Son for the sins of men, are accomplished facts. Nothing can blot these things out of the world's history or change them, and nothing can alter the change they made, or made possible, in the relationship of man to God.

In writing to the Ephesians about the unity of the Spirit, Paul speaks of this unity, or oneness, as being also an accomplished fact of the spiritual world. It already exists. "It is a gift of God which is committed to men to keep intact. At the same time . . . it is a unity which is ever enlarging its range and contents: 'until we all come to the unity.' The unity must be maintained in the process, if it is to be attained in the result."[23]

Disunity among races, nations, and men is very evident wherever we look in our present world. Even in the Church, the One Body of which Paul speaks, there is a lamentable lack of unity. If there is, underlying all the strife and disunity of the secular world, an essential, fundamental unity in the spiritual world, Christian people should surely know more about it and, at the same time, do more about it than most of them are doing.

An Established Reality

Human efforts to produce unity and peace among men by means of conferences, negotiations, and agreements are to be commended and encouraged. They are the reaching out from the secular level of life for something which men feel must exist somewhere in the universe. Though they never succeed completely, they never fail completely if, among those in charge, there are even a few choice spirits who place the good of humanity above the interests of a few.

The unity of which Paul writes, however, is not the result of any human effort. Rather, it is the unity which is produced by the Holy Spirit and is characteristic of His distinctive mission in God's redemptive plans. This is a Oneness which God, the Creator of the world and its order, has been working to make actual and permanent since the beginning. The struggles of men to find unity and peace are an unconscious effort to arise from the secular level of life to the spiritual level. Perhaps they would strive harder if they could know and believe that true unity, the unity of the Spirit, is already an established reality and can progressively be realized and brought into the actualities of life.

In our best, our quietest, our most Christian moments, we sometimes feel a bond of unity with all mankind. More often, we feel this bond of unity with those who are closest to us, or who are associated with us in a common task, or because of a common danger. The most satisfying experience a person ever has is that of coming so close to another in spirit that the two seem to understand each other without conscious effort, to love each other without thought of self, and to grow in spiritual stature while in each other's company. It is the work of the enemy of God and the enemy of our souls to mar such unity wherever it is found, to insinuate doubts of its reality, and to keep man as far away spiritually from his fellow man as possible.

Wherever real spiritual unity is experienced among men in this troubled world, there it is found that a little bit of heaven seems to have descended from above to dwell and manifest itself on earth. It is a blessed fact that there is always far more of such unity existing in this world of men than we know or realize. The one impression of the Ecumenical Conference held at Oxford, England, in 1937, which has remained most vivid in the mind of the writer, who was a delegate, is the extent and strength of Christian unity then existent over the world in the face of titanic forces of evil openly seeking to destroy it. The Second World War began with the "incident" of Shanghai Bridge even while the Conference was in session. Ten years later when the war clouds had lifted, the reality of Christian unity, so far from being destroyed by the forces of war, had been strengthened, and the World Council of Churches became an established fact.

Unity Must Be Kept

The unity which is an essential characteristic of the Spirit, and which is produced by the Spirit in the spiritual realm of life, must be kept intact by men whose hearts have been spiritually renewed. Paul wrote the Ephesians that they should endeavor to keep the unity of the Spirit in the bond of peace. The word used for "endeavor" has an eagerness and an urgency about it. The corresponding noun, found five times in II Corinthians, seventh and eighth chapters, is rendered in the King James Version by synonyms which attempt to bring out the meaning of this expressive word: "carefulness," "care," "diligence," "forwardness," "earnest care."

Christian people, Paul would say (see Ephesians 4:1), must earnestly strive, everywhere and all the time, to live worthy of their high calling in order to keep the unity of the Spirit and make it effective for the peace of the world. He does not leave anyone in doubt as to what kind of life he should live. It is a life of lowliness and meekness, long-suffering and forbearing love. These are character qualities which Paul lifted out of the life of Jesus. They were "foreshadowed in the lives of Spirit-inspired leaders of ancient times and . . . brought to full expression in the experience of Him whose life moved steadily and unfalteringly between the poles of reverent submission to the authority of God and adventurous purposeful relations with men."[24] Jesus, from the beginning of His life to the end, kept always the unity of the Spirit in the bond of peace, for He was given the Spirit without measure. His inner peace and outward majesty of bearing at every point of His life, and especially during His trials and crucifixion, was a proof of this fact and, at the same time, an illustration of its result.

Characteristics of a Life Which Keeps the Unity of the Spirit

In the matter of keeping the unity of the Spirit in the bond of peace, Paul does not seem to be so much concerned with what a man does in his life as how he does it. That is, the question of keeping the unity of the Spirit depends more on how life is lived than on what it accomplishes. The three character qualities he lists are as different from qualities of character valued by the world as are the Beatitudes of Jesus from the opinion of men regarding sources of happiness.

All Lowliness and Meekness

The first character quality listed is taken from the words of Jesus about Himself: "I am meek and lowly in heart." (Matthew 11:29.) Lowliness means true humility, and meekness means gentleness. They are different aspects of the same quality, describing the inner state of the heart.

Humility and gentleness have never been highly regarded in the world of men. Often they do not seem to be highly regarded in the Church by followers of Him who declared Himself to be meek and lowly in heart and who pronounced a blessing upon those who possess these qualities in their lives.

During the rapid rise of Nazism in Germany with its doctrines of force, hardness, and pitilessness, Dr. Emil Brunner, the great Swiss theologian, visited in Atlanta, Georgia. I asked him what was the German version of Philippians 4:5, which reads in part in our Bibles: "Let your moderation be known unto all men." He told me the German word for moderation and said that the English rendering would be: "Let your softness be known to all men." With the way to true greatness written down in its Bible as "softness," the German nation chose "hardness," and was destroyed. Interested in learning the rendering of this verse in the Bibles of other European nations, then torn with strife and war, I found that in the French Bible it was, "Let your sweetness be known to all men"; in the Spanish Bible, "Let your modesty be known to all men"; and in the Italian Bible, "Let your gentleness be known to all men."

With a Third World War threatening the peoples of the earth, those who believe in and accept the Gospel need surpassingly to remember the teachings of their Bibles, the example of their Saviour, and the experiences of the past. Pride and hardness, the opposites of humility and gentleness, may enforce an outward unity and peace for a while, but they weaken the unity of the Spirit, without which there can be no lasting peace in the hearts of men, or in the life of the world. Let us understand, however, that this does not mean that Christian people should passively submit to evil or acquiesce in the events of life whether good or

bad. The qualities of humility and gentleness can be more terrible and destroying when directed against evil than the opposite
qualities which are themselves always tainted by the evil they
seek to destroy.

Long-suffering, or Patience

The second characteristic which must be practiced in the life
of those who are endeavoring to keep the unity of the Spirit in
the bond of peace is long-suffering, or patience.

Impatience is often the besetting sin of an otherwise sincere
Christian. Lack of patience is generally characteristic of those
who know not Christ. This may, or may not, manifest itself in
an outward lack of self-control. Indeed, there are men of the
world who sometimes seem to possess more self-control than men
of the Church. Self-control in a Christian can better be expressed
as God-control — the letting go of self so that God may take
charge. A Christian who has placed his life under the control of
God is never factious, disagreeable, or insistent on having his
own way.

The patience of which Paul speaks, however, reaches beyond
our personal contacts. A Christian must be patient with the
long processes God uses in dealing with men, and with the
apparently small progress of the work He is carrying on in
us, and through us. In the vegetable world, as well as in the
animal world, growth can be forced and maturity hastened. We
are fond of using quick methods of producing vegetables and
fruit, and of getting poultry ready for the table. Unconsciously,
perhaps, we carry the same idea into the spiritual world, and
chafe at the failure of our efforts to hasten spiritual growth. The
prophet of old was much wiser in the ways of God when he gave
as the directive for work in the realm of the Spirit: "For precept
must be upon precept, precept upon precept; line upon line, line
upon line; here a little, and there a little." (Isaiah 28:10.)

Let us, as Christians, be patient and refuse to be discouraged
when it seems that progress is so small in the establishment of

God's Kingdom among men. Paul may plant and Apollos water, but it is God who giveth the increase. Our duty is to be faithful with the planting and watering, and to be patient in waiting for results to appear.

Loving Forbearance

Humility, gentleness, and patience are inner characteristics of the heart of a man who is filled with the Spirit. They inevitably show in outward conduct, for as a man thinketh in his heart, so is he. The third characteristic necessary for preserving the unity of the Spirit, as given by Paul, is loving forbearance — "forbearing one another in love." This applies in an unmistakable way to the human contacts which every man must have each day that he lives.

A lack of loving forbearance quickly destroys unity and peace in any gathering of men, and in any enterprise of life. The presence of this noble quality of character softens every contact of life. As sunshine acting on sensitive paper, it brings to view many beautiful and excellent things which would never have appeared without its influence. If this is true in the secular world, how much more true it is in the spiritual world. The failure of Christians to be forbearing toward one another is often amazing. How can we expect to keep the unity of the Spirit in the bond of peace if we have not learned to practice forbearance in love in our dealings with fellow Christians?

Loving forbearance is necessary each day in the experience of a Christian as he comes in contact with those outside the Christian family who do things contrary to his desires and opposed to his interests. Let us ever keep in mind the loving forbearance of our Master as He faced His enemies during the trials before both the ecclesiastical and the civil authorities, and the forbearance with which He bore on His shoulders the cross upon which they were soon to crucify Him. If He had shown an attitude which indicated a lack of humility, gentleness, and patience in His heart, and loving forbearance in His conduct, there would have been no atonement made for sin, and therefore no hope for you and me. Jesus won the victory and triumphed gloriously. Dare we neglect the qualities of character He possessed in His work of bringing many sons to glory, as we face the Gethsemanes of our day?

The Unity of the Spirit Becoming Actual

The unity of the Spirit underlies the fellowship of the Spirit and the communion of saints, both of which manifest and interpret it. This will be further explained in the following chapter. Here, let it be noted that if peace is a consummation devoutly to be wished in this world, the way to peace lies in the progressive actualization in life of the unity of the Spirit. Perhaps this is not the kind of peace we have been seeking. It only incidentally includes prosperity and worldly happiness, if it includes them at all. It is not an antidote for many of the common ills of life. It leaves unsolved many problems which past centuries have grappled with and which future centuries will find still on the agenda of humanity. It does not do for us what we can and should be doing for ourselves. It does, however, bring quiet strength and confidence to our inward life, which enables us to look out upon the world with clearer vision, greater moral courage, and firmer faith.

This peace is not only the result of keeping the unity of the Spirit, it is also the accompanying means by which it is kept. "As much as lieth in you," wrote Paul in Romans 12:18, "live peaceably with all men." The measure of the ability that lies within us to live peaceably with all men is the measure of the unity of the Spirit we have kept by means of humility, gentleness, patience, and loving forbearance.

Christianity has been called an impractical thing, an idealistic code out of the reach of men, a grand idea unattainable in this life. The ideas, ideals, and methods of the world are supposed to be attainable and practical. Even so, consider what these ideals and methods have done to men and to the life of nations and peoples. Are we forced to accept ideas or to continue to use methods which have already resulted in failure and loss?

In this atomic age, when the sands of time are rapidly running out, surely we should begin to take seriously the teaching of the Holy Scriptures, and the example of our blessed Lord! Have faith in God, and in the long but unfailing processes by means of which He brings to pass His loving purposes of redemption.

Chapter 10

THE COMMUNION OF SAINTS ACTIVATED

"Be not conformed to this world: but be ye transformed by the renewing of your mind." — ROMANS 12:2.

THE APOSTOLIC BENEDICTION, with which Paul's second letter to the Corinthians closes, pronounces a threefold blessing upon believers: the grace of the Lord Jesus Christ, the love of God, and the communion, or fellowship, of the Holy Spirit. Christians who are more or less instructed in the meaning of the phrases, "grace of the Lord Jesus Christ" and "the love of God," often have only a faint or hazy idea of what the fellowship of the Holy Spirit means. Since the work of each Person of the Trinity is essential in the salvation of men and in the building of Christ's Kingdom, the neglect of one phase of that work is dangerous, and may prove disastrous.

The unity of the Spirit, discussed in the preceding chapter, is a somewhat abstract term, of which the fellowship of the Spirit is the outward or concrete manifestation. The unity of the Spirit underlies the fellowship of the Spirit. The two are inward and outward aspects of the same work of divine grace.

The Fellowship of the Spirit

The term, fellowship of the Spirit, as used by the New Testament writers, may mean either the fellowship a believer can have with the Holy Spirit, or the fellowship the Holy Spirit produces among believers. Or it may mean both at the same time. That is, the meaning may be subjective, or objective, or both subjective and objective. It is not necessary to try to separate the two meanings, save in an effort to understand the term better.

Dr. A. J. Gordon in his book, *The Ministry of the Spirit*, places under the general head "The Communion of the Spirit" the three great works of divine grace in the heart and life of a man:

1. The Spirit of Life: Our Regeneration.
2. The Spirit of Holiness: Our Sanctification.
3. The Spirit of Glory: Our Transfiguration.

The Holy Spirit, writes Dr. Gordon, makes true in us what is already true for us through the saving work of our blessed Lord. This seems to be very close to the meaning of John's words in his First Epistle: "Truly our fellowship is with the Father, and with his Son Jesus Christ. . . . if we walk in the light, as he is in the light, we have fellowship one with another, and the blood of Jesus Christ his Son cleanseth us from all sin." (I John 1:3, 7.)

The fellowship of the Holy Spirit, in its subjective meaning, is an expressive way of representing, or picturing, the new life of a Christian as he turns away from the "weak and beggarly elements" of the world to seek and enjoy the all-satisfying fellowship with God the Father, and with Jesus Christ the Son, which is made available for him. The Holy Spirit is the author of this fellowship, and the one who bestows and sustains it. Without the work of the Spirit, there could be no application of the redemption purchased by Christ.

If the question be asked whether a Christian can do anything to assure or to strengthen that relationship with his Maker and Redeemer which is described in the term fellowship of the Spirit,

the answer can surely be found in I Corinthians 12:3, "Wherefore I give you to understand, that no man speaking by the Spirit
of God calleth Jesus accursed: and that no man can say that
Jesus is the Lord, but by the Holy Ghost." It is as simple and as
profound as that. When a man sincerely confesses Jesus Christ as
his Lord, he is "caught up into a new experience of fellowship
which is none other than the fellowship of the Holy Spirit."
Whenever he expresses loyalty to Christ and His cause in the
words he speaks, the service he renders, or the life he lives, the
Spirit works powerfully within him to strengthen the divine
fellowship.

ONE BODY AND ONE SPIRIT

Following his exhortation to keep the unity of the Spirit in the
bond of peace (Ephesians 4:3), Paul enforces his argument by
reminding the members of the church at Ephesus that they are
one body and one spirit. The one body is ultimately indistin-
guishable from the Body of Christ, and the one spirit from the
Holy Spirit. But, just as the fellowship of the saints is the outward
manifestation of the unity of the Spirit, so the one body, or
church, to which believers belong, and the one spirit which ani-
mates that body, are the concrete actualization of the Body of
Christ, and of the Holy Spirit. Referring to the paraphrase of
Ephesians 4:1-6, which is found at the beginning of the preceding chapter, we read: "Oneness is characteristic of the Gospel.
Consider its present working and its predestined issue: there is
one Body, animated by one Spirit . . . "

It is the grand conception of Paul that the Church is the Body
of Christ on earth, His continuing incarnation among men, and
that the Holy Spirit dwells in that Body and gives it life. This
Church is not limited by time or space. It is most certainly not
to be identified with any existing church whether Roman
Catholic or Protestant, or with any denomination. It is the
Church Invisible made up of all true Christians of every age
and land, past, present, and future. Of this Body, Christ is the
Head in heaven.

The relationship of the Head to the Body is first of all that of authority. Christ as the Head is the one, supreme authority of the Church. Whenever a church does not recognize this authority or substitutes someone or something for it, that church ceases to be a part of the Body of Christ. The Head is also the source of all needed graces to the Church — wisdom, guidance, strength, ultimate victory. The gifts of Christ to the Church are for the equipment of the saints, the work of the ministry, and the building up of the Body of Christ. (See Ephesians 4:12, R.S.V.)

The Visible Church, the church we see and know, "consists of all those throughout the world that profess the true religion, together with their children." Paul made no distinction between the Invisible and the Visible Church, and we do not need to do so save that we may understand that the Invisible Church is without spot, or wrinkle, or any such thing, while the Visible Church does not now possess such perfectness, or completeness, but is yet in the process of being "built up." Protestant churches, recognizing this distinction, have within themselves the principle and power of continual correction of errors and refreshment of life. Non-Protestant churches, identifying the Kingdom of God on earth with their own organizations, do not have this vital life-giving principle and consequently perpetuate and enlarge their errors.

The Communion of Saints

A study of the teachings of Jesus provides abundant evidence for the belief that whatever human organization He intended should be formed after His earthly life was over, it should be, first of all, a brotherhood, a fraternity, or a group in spiritual fellowship. He gave no new command save that the disciples should love one another even as He had loved them. He prayed that believers might be one, "as thou, Father, art in me, and I in thee, that they also may be one in us." (John 17:21.) He warned the Apostles against following the way of the Gentiles in seeking places of prominence and authority, and then astonished them by saying: "It shall not be so among you: but whosoever will be great among you, let him be your minister; and whosoever will be chief among you, let him be your servant." (Matthew 20:26-27.)

After Pentecost, the place and need of fellowship among believers, which Jesus had taught, was made effective in the lives of the disciples by the work of the Holy Spirit. "The early Christian community, as Luke describes it [in the book of Acts], exhibited a conscious unity, a warm sympathy among its members, a fellowship of love, and a generous relief of each other's needs. They 'were of one heart and soul: and not one of them said that aught of the things which he possessed was his own; but they had all things common.' The word that expresses all this is 'koinonia,' translated in our version fellowship or communion, and representing one of the great ideas of the New Testament."[25]

Paul, whose writings did most to develop the idea of the Church, continually exhorted Christians to walk worthy of their calling. The brethren were to love each other, to be like-minded, to esteem the things of others more highly than their own, and not to take their disputes to heathen law courts for settlement. Peter does not use the word church at all, but rather the word brotherhood. "Honour all men. Love the brotherhood. Fear God. Honour the king." (I Peter 2:17.) John uses the word church only in his Third Epistle, but speaks often of the brethren. His test for assurance of salvation should be written on the hearts of all Christians: "We know that we have passed from death unto life, because we love the brethren." (I John 3:14.) In this test, he has followed the words of his Master: "By this shall all men know that ye are my disciples, if ye have love one to another." (John 13:35.) The neglect of brotherly love and Christian fellowship by the Church and in the churches, from the days of the Apostles down to our own time, has been a costly departure from Scriptural teaching.

The Communion of Saints Activated

Worldly conformity is a well-known expression in church terminology, though it is not heard so much in our day as in former years. Perhaps the reason is that our fathers too largely identified worldly conformity with the act of engaging in certain amusements which, in their day, were frowned upon by the Church. They may have been right in their instinctive disapproval of these amusements, which for the sake of charity will not be named here, but wrong in the reasons they gave for condemnation. However that may be, the tragic truth of the situation was that those who sat in condemnation were often more guilty of worldly conformity, as Paul used the term in Romans 12:2, than those who were condemned. Worldly conformity is permitting the spirit of the age at the time a Christian is living to control him, to dominate him, and to make him live according to the standards the world has set up.

The entire twelfth chapter of Romans may be viewed as an exposition of worldly conformity contrasted with heavenly conformity. It clearly presents the conduct of those animated by the spirit of the age and the lives of those guided by the Spirit of God. The way of the world is the way of selfishness, self-seeking, bitterness, hatred, wrath, evil-speaking, and malice. The world condemns sins of the flesh, such as murder, adultery, and stealing, but often holds in high esteem those who are guilty of sins of disposition. When such an attitude and spirit appears in the life of a Christian, it is worldly conformity and plays havoc with the communion of saints.

The way of Christ is the way of unselfishness — love, joy, peace, long-suffering, gentleness, goodness, faith, meekness, and temperance. These qualities of life, Paul points out in Galatians 5:22-23, are the fruit of the Spirit. Many church members, judging from their lives, do not believe very strongly that such qualities of character are important, or even desirable. Others have never suspected that the lack of these qualities and the presence of their opposites in the life of a Christian are clear evidence of worldly conformity.

It is highly significant that the verb translated "be ye transformed" in Romans 12:2 is not in the passive voice but, rather, in the middle voice which is peculiar to the Greek language. The middle voice is used to denote action upon one's self. Paul really wrote, "Transform yourselves by the renewing of your mind." The believer, being already regenerated, co-operates with the Holy Spirit in this work and needs to be urged to holy activity. The same thought and command is here that Paul wrote the Ephesians when he told them to "put off . . . the old man, which is corrupt," and to be "renewed in the spirit of your mind," and "put on the new man, which after God is created in righteousness and true holiness." (See Ephesians 4:22-24.)

Worldly conformity, as set forth above, is the worst enemy of the communion of saints. Transforming ourselves by the renewing of our minds so that we may do the will of God and produce a life that is good, and acceptable, and perfect or well-rounded, strengthens the communion of saints and activates it. As children grow and develop character according to the atmosphere of the home into which they are born, so those who are "born again" grow and develop a type of Christian life which is conditioned by the atmosphere of the church to which they belong. If the church's spiritual atmosphere is cold and the fellowship of the saints is weak, new members who are added to the church have small chance of becoming mature Christians.

A warm atmosphere of Christian fellowship gives life and vitality to the worship and service of a church. Without it, the best efforts to "enrich" worship and to increase service activities will be empty and ineffectual. With it, worshipers can be brought close to God and workers made into effective witnesses for Christ even though an adequate building and equipment are lacking and organizational efficiency is noticeably absent. The very first thing a church should do when a new member is received is to bring that member into the warm center of its fellowship. If it does not do this, the member may remain on the fringes of the congregation and in due time be lost out the "back door" of the church.

The power of Christian fellowship enables the Church and the individual members thereof to face a hostile and sinful world and apply to it in an effective way the saving power of the Gospel. It is well to remember that the Apostles had been taught and trained by Jesus Himself, yet they remained inactive and power-less after Jesus' departure until they were welded into a Christian fellowship by the outpouring of the Holy Spirit. From that time on, they were invincible. Individually every one of them was expendable, but collectively as a fellowship in the church they were triumphant.

There is no way of totaling or reporting an increase of Christian fellowship in a church at the end of a fiscal year. I wish there were. I wish that numbers added and money raised might cease to be the standards by which the effectiveness of a church is judged, and that churches could be encouraged and urged to give their best efforts to the increase of Christian fellowship among their members. In the warm atmosphere of Christian fellowship, problems both ecclesiastical and personal have a way of disappearing, effectiveness in worship and service grows in leaps and bounds, and there comes to the members of the fellowship joy unspeakable and full of glory.

Chapter 11

JOY UNSPEAKABLE AND FULL OF GLORY

"For the kingdom of God is not meat and drink; but righteousness,
and peace, and joy in the Holy Ghost." — ROMANS 14:17.

IF THERE IS A JOY unspeakable and full of glory for believers — using Peter's phrase in I Peter 1:8 — anywhere to be
had in this weary world, surely we, as Christians, ought to
know more about it. Common observation, or even diligent
search, does not reveal very much evidence of genuine joy in the
Church, and certainly not out of it. As the Christians of Ephesus, when asked by Paul whether they had received the Holy
Spirit since they believed, replied, "We have not so much as
heard whether there be any Holy Spirit" (Acts 19:2), so church
members today might reply to a similar question concerning
Christian joy: "We have not so much as heard whether there be
any Christian joy."

"To the law and to the testimony: if they speak not according to this word, it is because there is no light in them." (Isaiah
8:20.)*

---

*This verse is quoted out of its context for the sake of spiritual truth it expresses when
standing alone.

Joy in the Bible

Many years ago, when I was a Seminary student, a copy of Dr. Fosdick's devotional classic, *The Manhood of the Master,* came into my hands. The deep impression made by the first chapter, entitled "The Master's Joy," has remained with me to this day, when all the other chapters have been forgotten. The human joyfulness of Jesus during His life on earth was something that had never been called to my attention before. It was, and has continued to be, an inspiring thought that Jesus, though He was a man of sorrows and acquainted with grief, had inner resources of joy that outer circumstances and experiences could not touch. In His last intimate "conference" with His disciples in the upper room, He expressed His deep desire to pass this joy on to His followers: "These things have I spoken unto you, that my joy might remain in you, and that your joy might be full." (John 15:11.)

Though the Old Testament might not be called a joyful book, yet the words "joy" and "rejoice" are found often enough on its pages. God is said to rejoice over His people when they are in fellowship with Him (see Deuteronomy 30:9, and especially Zephaniah 3:17), and the joy of the Lord is their strength (Nehemiah 8:10). The book of Psalms, the hymnbook of the Hebrew people, is a book of joy.

It is the New Testament, however, that Dr. Fosdick called the most joyful book in the world. "It opens with joy over the birth of Jesus; and it ends with a superb picture of a multitude which no man could number, singing Hallelujah Choruses. No matter where you open it, amid fortunate or discouraging circumstances, you always hear the note of joy."[26] Following this lead I examined all the passages concerning joy in the New Testament, and was amazed to find that the majority of these passages related joy to some type of human suffering. Selected examples are here given:

Joy in persecution: "And they departed from the presence of the council, rejoicing that they were counted worthy to suffer shame for his name." (Acts 5:41.)

Joy in trial: "Beloved, think it not strange concerning the fiery trial which is to try you, as though some strange thing happened unto you: but rejoice, inasmuch as ye are partakers of Christ's sufferings; that, when his glory shall be revealed, ye may be glad also with exceeding joy." (I Peter 4:12-13.)

Joy in financial loss: "For ye had compassion of me in my bonds, and took joyfully the spoiling of your goods, knowing in yourselves that ye have in heaven a better and an enduring substance." (Hebrews 10:34.)

Joy in poverty: "How that in a great trial of affliction the abundance of their joy and their deep poverty abounded unto the riches of their liberality." (II Corinthians 8:2.)

Joy in sorrow: "As sorrowful, yet always rejoicing. . . ." (II Corinthians 6:10, a.s.v.)

Joy in all circumstances of life: "Rejoice in the Lord alway: and again I say, Rejoice." (Philippians 4:4.)

The source of all true joy for the New Testament Christian is the Holy Spirit. Paul uses the phrase, "joy of the Holy Spirit" in I Thessalonians 1:6, and the phrase, "joy in the Holy Spirit" in Romans 14:17. The Holy Spirit rejoices in His joyful ministry and enables Christians who are in fellowship with Him to be joyful in their life and work. Only true children of God can rejoice when they are counted worthy to suffer for Christ. "Their joy is in some sense a present recompense for their sufferings; but for suffering they could not know it."[27]

Causes of Lack of Joy

Studdert-Kennedy, English poet-preacher of the First World War, wrote:

> "Peace does not mean the end of all our striving,
>   Joy does not mean the drying of our tears;
>   Peace is the power that comes to souls arriving
>   Up to the light where God Himself appears.
>
> "Joy is the wine that God is ever pouring
>   Into the hearts of those who strive with Him,
>   Lightening their eyes to vision and adoring,
>   Strengthening their arms to warfare glad and grim."[28]

Perhaps one of the reasons that the followers of Jesus know so little of Christian joy in their lives is that they have utterly misunderstood what it is. The Beatitudes, or Happinesses, Jesus pronounced upon certain types of His disciples have never been taken seriously by His followers, or, at least, have left them unconvinced. (See Matthew 5:3-12.) As a result, we find those in our churches who look upon any demonstration or experience of happiness on the part of a Christian with suspicion, and even with disapproval. The long-faced, gloomy type of church member who stands ready to rebuke joy and happiness whenever it appears in his church is doubtless not unknown to readers of this book. This is just as true among Presbyterians as among members of other denominations; Presbyterians, who have as the answer to the first question of their Shorter Catechism: "Man's chief end is to glorify God, and to enjoy Him forever." How can man enjoy God who is unseen unless he enjoys Him in the things He has made which are seen?

However, it would be a mistake to think that joy in the Holy Spirit is dependent upon things we see and experiences we have. It is not at all a matter of satisfying our physical senses or our human desires in the way the world apart from Christ seeks satisfaction. "A good man shall be satisfied from himself." (Proverbs 14:14.) Sources of joy are found within a man's heart rather than without. Many rich and apparently fortunate men are very unhappy. Many who occupy places of prominence and fame in the world would be willing to exchange their lot for a more humble one if they could then be assured of peace of mind and joy of heart. The attainment of riches is too often accompanied or followed by broken hearts, and the attainment of power by broken health. The poet Wordsworth was close to reality when he wrote:

> "The world is too much with us; late and soon,
> Getting and spending, we lay waste our powers."[29]

This is often just as true of Christian people as of non-Christians. The joy which the world gives — coming, as John says, in response to the lust of the flesh, the lust of the eyes, and the pride of life — passes away. Only he that doeth the will of the Father abideth forever, and the joy he finds in doing that will cannot be taken away from him. (See I John 2:16-17.)

Since Christian joy is a by-product of fellowship with the Spirit, another reason for lack of joy in the life of a follower of Jesus is unwillingness to pay the price, or fulfill the conditions, of such fellowship. The warnings of Paul to the Ephesians not to grieve the Holy Spirit (Ephesians 4:30) and to the Thessalonians (I Thessalonians 5:19) not to quench the Spirit indicate that this fellowship may be hindered, interrupted, or even destroyed. Bitterness, wrath, anger, clamor, evil speaking, and malice grieve the Spirit. (See Ephesians 4:30-31.) Lack of complete dedication to Christ quenches the Spirit. Though Jesus loved the rich young ruler, He never entered into spiritual fellowship with him because this man, possessed of great wealth and unwilling to dedicate it to Jesus, went away sorrowful from the Prince of Life. (See Mark 10:21-22.)

What is there in your life or in mine that grieves or quenches the Spirit? Whatever it is, we had better give it up and get rid of it or we will never know Christian joy.

Growing in Joy

If a man who has made his confession of faith in Christ has never received the Holy Spirit's gift of joy, how can it be obtained? Or if he has it only in part, how can joy be made to grow, or increase? Before attempting an answer to these questions, I would like to point out that Christian joy is not a heavenly blessing within reach of only a few choice saints, or attained by use of a magic formula or in any strange and unusual way. As Paul pointed out when writing to the Romans about righteousness by faith, the Gospel does not require impossibilities of those who accept it, such as scaling the heavens or fathoming the great abyss. It asks only cordial faith and open acknowledgment, or confession, for the knowledge of God's will in every matter of faith and life has been made perfectly accessible to believers. (See Romans 10:6-9.) Putting into practice under the guidance of the Holy Spirit that portion of God's will for us that we know, is the first and second and every subsequent step in the attainment of divine joy. The way ever opens up before us, as we go forward. Three guideposts for spiritual pilgrims who are seeking increase of joy in their lives are given below.

Forsaking All Sin

Those who sought membership in the communion to which the writer belongs were formerly asked, among other questions, this very searching one: "Do you now resolve and promise, in humble reliance upon the grace of the Holy Spirit, that you will endeavor to walk [live] as becometh the followers of Christ, forsaking all sin, and conforming your life to His teaching and example?" A revision was made in this question, some years ago, which omitted the phrase, "forsaking all sin." This was doubtless done because the revisers thought that a man can't forsake all sin. Certainly that is true, but he can never be released from his Christian duty of trying earnestly to forsake every sin that he knows he is committing. The Gospel message is that a man can be saved from sin and not that he can be saved in sin.

The Fifty-first Psalm, one of the finest and most touching passages of Scripture, describes David's agony of repentance following his great sin against God, against Israel, and against Uriah, and his search for restoration to God's favor. Verses ten through twelve of the Psalm express the prayer of a man who has forsaken his sin and realizes what God must do for him before he can ever again be happy.

> "Create in me a clean heart, O God;
>   And renew a right spirit within me.
>
> "Cast me not away from thy presence;
>   And take not thy holy Spirit from me.
>
> "Restore unto me the joy of thy salvation;
>   And uphold me with a willing spirit." (A.S.V.)

Dr. Maclaren in his exposition of this Psalm wrote this comment on the verses just quoted: "What is 'Thy salvation' but the gift of a clean heart and a steadfast spirit, the blessed consciousness of unbroken closeness of communion with God, in which the suppliant suns himself in the beams of God's face, and receives an uninterrupted communication of His Spirit's gifts? These are the sources of pure joy, lasting as God Himself, and victorious over all occasions for surface sorrow."[30]

Dedication of Heart and Life

The need for complete dedication of a man's heart and life before he can become a true follower of Jesus has already been mentioned. As long as a Christian has a divided allegiance, there can be no joy or satisfaction in his life and service. "If any man will come after me, let him deny himself, and take up his cross, and follow me." (Matthew 16:24.) Life out of death, strength out of weakness, joy out of sorrow — these are the promises of the Master to those who follow Him all the way. The Kingdom of God, which Jesus proclaimed, is not meat and drink, nor power and success, but righteousness, and peace, and joy in the Holy Spirit. (See Romans 14:17.)

Enlistment and Service in a Great Cause

Since joy is a by-product of the Christian life and warfare against sin, and is never found by a direct search, it must come from being zealous for the Master's cause and fervent in spirit as we serve the Lord. The James-Lange theory of the emotions may not be entirely true, but it has long intrigued me and it seems to point the way to the possession of Christian joy. The theory, in brief, is that men feel because they act rather than act because they feel. For example, a man is sad because he sheds tears and not, as is generally thought, sad before he sheds tears. I am angry at a man because I hit him, and do not first become angry and afterward hit him. Boys engage in a tussle which is likely to end up in a fight. They have been going through the motions of fighting and those motions produce anger. Worshipers in church have often been surprised and pleased when they assumed an attitude of reverence and later found that they felt a reverence which had not been theirs before they acted reverently.

Without taking the theory too seriously, it ought to help us to realize that enlistment in a great cause and activitiy in advancing that cause is the surest known way to happiness and satisfaction in life. That which is true in part in the secular world is true in a more complete sense in the religious world. Too often church members who have made a profession of their faith in Christ and their loyalty to Him do not follow their profession with activity and service for Christ in the church and in the world. Their Christian life and experience remain static and the joy of salvation cannot be bestowed upon them by the Holy Spirit. Let them once forget, or deny, themselves and begin following the Master in the path of service and suffering, and they will be surprised at the dawning of joy in their hearts and at its steady increase. It is the joy of the Holy Spirit to give joy to those for whom it has been prepared, and who are themselves prepared to receive it.

"These things have I spoken unto you, that my joy might remain in you, and that your joy might be full." (John 15:11.) As Paul speaks of the peace of God that passes understanding (Philippians 4:7), so Peter speaks of joy unspeakable and full of glory (I Peter 1:8). It can't be expressed in words but it can be experienced in life. In the midst of the tribulations of the world, which Jesus warned His followers they should expect, the Holy Spirit bestows upon God's faithful children the joy of their Lord.

> "Jesus, Thou Joy of loving hearts,
> Thou Fount of life, Thou Light of men,
> From the best bliss that earth imparts
> We turn unfilled to Thee again."[31]

Chapter 12

PENTECOST, THEN AND NOW

> "This spake he of the Spirit, which they that believe on him should receive: for the Holy Ghost was not yet given; because that Jesus was not yet glorified." — JOHN 7:39.
>
> "And when the day of Pentecost was fully come . . ." — ACTS 2:1.

PERHAPS NO SCRIPTURAL DOCTRINE has suffered so from neglect as the doctrine of the Holy Spirit and His work. This neglect has been of incalculable loss to the Christian Church, and to Christians individually. Many church members who have faithfully attended the preaching services of their churches might honestly say, as did those "certain disciples" of old at Ephesus: "We have not so much as heard whether there be any Holy Spirit." (See Acts 19:2.)

If the Church is ever to recapture the power and the enthusiasm which characterized the lives of the early Christians, set forth so clearly in the New Testament, it must turn its attention more seriously to the revealed source of that power and enthusiasm. Perhaps it is true, as has been said, that Christians today are more like the disciples before Pentecost than the disciples after Pentecost. "Prior to Pentecost, they had been, for the most part, instructed disciples. After Pentecost, they were inspired disciples."[32]

The historic Church needs also to rescue this doctrine from the mistreatment it is receiving at the hands of certain modern and more or less fanatical groups who, sensing the need for an emphasis on the doctrine of the Holy Spirit which it was not receiving, have handled it with a zeal which is commendable but not according to knowledge. Rather than being prejudiced against the Holy Spirit and His work by the weird and fanatical teachings and actions of some groups, serious Christians would do well to seek for elements of refreshing vitality in their demonstrations and then turn to the law and to the testimony for correction of errors and instruction in positive righteousness.

The Birthday of the Spirit

Augustine, the great theologian of Alexandria in Egypt (354-430 A.D.), called the Day of Pentecost the "dies natalis," or birthday, of the Holy Spirit. The words which begin the narrative of the descent of the Spirit, "And when the day of Pentecost was fully come" (Acts 2:1), are similar to the words of Paul as he writes the Galatians about the incarnation of Christ: "When the fulness of the time was come, God sent forth his Son" (Galatians 4:4).

The day on which Mary brought forth her first-born Son we call the birthday of Christ, or Christmas. Now when we speak of the birthday of Christ we do not mean that He came into existence on that day. He was in the beginning with God. He was the agent in creation. "All things were made by him; and without him was not any thing made that was made." (John 1:3.) He was the mysterious "Angel of the Lord," or "Angel of the Covenant," of whose appearance frequent mention is made in the Old Testament. On the day of His birth, the Second Person of the Trinity became incarnate and entered into His ministry of revealing God to men and of making Himself a sacrificial offering for the sins of the world.

In a similar way the Holy Spirit existed, and His work is frequently mentioned in the Bible before the memorable Day of

Pentecost when He was "poured out on all flesh." As in the Old
Testament the Second Person of the Trinity is called the Angel
of the Lord, so the Third Person of the Trinity is called the
Spirit of the Lord. At the baptism of Jesus, the Gospels tell us
the Spirit descended from heaven like a dove, and abode upon
the Saviour. (See John 1:32.) But it was on the Day of Pentecost that the Holy Spirit entered into His distinctive ministry on
earth. The Spirit, "though given in His fullness to Christ Himself
(John 3:34), and operating through Him in His people (John
6:63), was not, until after Christ's return to glory, to be given to
the faithful as the Paraclete [Comforter] and representative of
Christ for the carrying on of His work."[33]

The divine order in the plan of redemption was that Christ's
work on earth should be completed and He, Himself, return to
the Father, and that then the Holy Spirit should be sent to apply
to the hearts and lives of men the redemption wrought out by
Christ and thus carry Christ's work to completion. This is the
meaning of John's words at the head of this chapter: "The Holy
Ghost was not yet given; because that Jesus was not yet glorified."
The divine order was prefigured in the worship of the Temple
where the altar of sacrifice and burnt offering came before the
laver, or basin of water, at which the priests washed and purified
themselves before officiating in the Temple worship. There was
also divine significance in the fact that Pentecost was the day
the Holy Spirit was given. Pentecost, or the Feast of Weeks, was
one of the three great annual Jewish religious festivals. It was
celebrated fifty days after the Feast of the Passover, and was also
called the Feast of Harvest because the first fruits of the harvest,
then ended, were presented by the people in the Temple. In
accordance with the order of sequence Paul, who wrote, "For
even Christ our passover is sacrificed for us" (I Corinthians 5:7),
also wrote: "But now is Christ risen from the dead, and become
the firstfruits of them that slept" (I Corinthians 15:20).

"And when the day of Pentecost was fully come" means,
therefore, more than a schedule of time completed. It means
that in God's plan of salvation the fullness of time was come for

the ministry of the Spirit to begin. "Christ having reached His goal, and not till then, bequeaths to His followers the graces that invested His earthly course; the ascending Elijah leaves His mantle behind Him. It is only an extension of the same principle, that the declared office of the Holy Spirit being to complete the image of Christ in every faithful follower by effecting in this world a spiritual death and resurrection, — a point attested in every epistle, — *the image could not be stamped until the reality had been wholly accomplished; the Divine Artist could not fitly descend to make the copy before the entire original had been provided.*"[34]

PERSONALITY OF THE SPIRIT

Perhaps one of the reasons that Christians who universally celebrate the birth of Christ each year give so little attention to Pentecost, the birthday of the Spirit, is that they do not fully understand or believe that the Spirit is a Person. It is not enough to believe that the Holy Spirit is a divine power and influence operating in the world and in the hearts of men. "There are three *persons* in the Godhead: the Father, the Son, and the Holy Ghost; and these three are one God, the same in substance, equal in power and glory." (See Shorter Catechism, Question 6.)

The inspired writers of the New Testament obviously believed that He was a Person, for they speak of Him as a Person, assign personal actions to Him, and narrate relationships with Him that can only exist between persons. He speaks (Acts 1:16); He performs miracles (Acts 2:4; 8:39); He gives orders and forbids actions (Acts 8:29; 16:6); He sets ministers over churches (Acts 20:28); He witnesses (Romans 8:16); Christians are warned not to grieve Him (Ephesians 4:30); He can be resisted (Acts 7:51); blasphemy against Him is unforgivable (Matthew 12:31-32).

A Christian to whom Jesus Christ is a living, personal reality will find that when the Holy Spirit also becomes to him a living, personal reality his life will have been made more complete, "stablished, strengthened, and settled" (see I Peter 5:10), than he has ever before known or believed possible.

THE NAME OF THE HOLY SPIRIT

The Saviour was named by the angel of the Lord before birth in a dream which Joseph had: "Thou shalt call his name JESUS: for he shall save his people from their sins." (See Matthew 1:18-21.) The Holy Spirit was named by Jesus in His last intimate talk with the Apostles before His arrest. The name "Comforter" appears in the fourteenth, fifteenth, and sixteenth chapters of John. This name is a translation of the Greek word used by Jesus. Perhaps it is not a happy translation for our day since the word "comfort" does not have for us the strong, positive meaning that it had in the days when the King James Version was made. More modern translations use the words "Counselor," "Advocate," "Helper."

Since the name Jesus is a transliteration of the Greek name used in the New Testament, it might have made the Holy Spirit more personal and real to us if we had learned to call Him by the transliteration of His Greek name, Paraclete. Doubtless this will now never be done, but it is well to know that the word itself means one who is always ready to be called to the Christian's aid. The Holy Spirit is the Christian's side-partner. Further than that, He "dwelleth with you, and shall be in you." (See John 14:17.)

THE BIRTHDAY OF THE CHURCH

Pentecost also marks the birthday of the Christian Church. As Jesus existed before He was born in Bethlehem of Judea, and the Holy Spirit existed before the Day of Pentecost which followed the death, resurrection, and ascension of Christ, so the Church existed before the Holy Spirit was given. In the Old Testament we find a foreshadow of the Church that was still in the future. Stephen, in his apologia, spoke of the church in the wilderness. (Acts 7:38.) In the Septuagint, which is the Greek translation of the Old Testament made in the third century B.C., the same word which is translated church in the New Testament is frequently used for the religious assemblies of Israel. But it was at Pentecost that the Church was commissioned, empowered, and started out on its triumphant mission in the world.

There are some Bible teachers who speak of the Church as the incarnation of the Spirit. However, it is better to think of the Church as the embodiment of the Spirit and at the same time the continuing incarnation of Christ on earth of which He is the Head in heaven. "The Holy Spirit not only dwells in the church as His habitation, but also uses her as the living organism whereby He moves and walks forth in the world, and speaks to the world, and acts upon the world. He is the soul of the church which is Christ's body."[35]

The time of the advent of the Spirit came ten days after the ascension of Jesus. The Apostles, in obedience to the command of Jesus, had waited in Jerusalem during those days in prayer and expectation. We are told in Acts 1:14 just who were with them in the upper room — "the women, and Mary the mother of Jesus, and his brethren." It does not follow that the gathering of the one hundred and twenty disciples to whom Peter proposed the election of a successor to Judas was held in the same upper room, which, being a loft of a private dwelling, could scarcely accommodate such a crowd. On the Day of Pentecost when they were all together in one place, there must have been a greater number present than the one hundred and twenty, and the place must have been the outer court of the Temple. This alone could accommodate the multitude that came together when the strange news of what was happening was noised abroad. And what more appropriate place could there have been for the commissioning of the new Church than that which had been known for centuries as the Temple, or House, of God?

The giving of the law to Moses on Mount Sinai was accompanied by awe-inspiring physical signs. (See Hebrews 12:18-21.) The birth of Jesus was announced by an angel and the song of a multitude of the heavenly host. It would have been strange if the advent of the Spirit had not been accompanied by physical phenomena and symbols. The sound of "a rushing mighty wind" was an echo of a mighty breath sweeping along, and the "cloven tongues like as of fire" were tongues as it were of fire passing from one to another and being distributed among them. David Smith suggests that the disciples were apart from the crowd in the court of the Temple and that attention was centered upon them, after the sound of the rushing mighty wind was heard, by the inspired change wrought in these disciples, who began speaking boldly and clearly so that everyone present could hear and understand what they said. The crowd could hear the wind's noise but they could not see the tongues of flame, just as later those who were with Paul on the journey to Damascus could hear the sound of the voice speaking to him but saw no man. (Acts 9:7.)

The change wrought in the disciples themselves was even more significant than the physical symbols. They had been told by the Saviour to wait in Jerusalem until they should be given power from on high by the coming of the Spirit. (Acts 1:4, 8.) That power being given and received, the little group of confused, fearful, and timid disciples were welded into the Christian Church whose members were utterly transformed from their former condition of mind, and heart, and life. Certain characteristics immediately emerged which set these men and women apart from any group of people the world had ever before seen or known. These characteristics have been diluted during the centuries after Pentecost, and sometimes seem to have been entirely lost. When, however, they appear in the Church and flourish in the lives of its members, power from on high is found again to be present and the Church continues her forward march.

UNITY

Before Pentecost, the disciples were individual believers in Christ and His Gospel. After Pentecost they were a unified body of believers. "The multitude of them that believed were of one heart and of one soul." (Acts 4:32.) It was this kind of unity Jesus prayed for in the seventeenth chapter of John: "That they all may be one; as thou, Father, art in me, and I in thee, that they also may be one in us: that the world may believe that thou hast sent me." (John 17:21.) It is this kind of unity that the Church must have today if it is to be effective in carrying out the marching orders of the Risen Lord. (See Matthew 28:19-20; Acts 1:8.)

The characteristics of this unity have been explained in detail in the ninth chapter.

EVERY MEMBER A WITNESS FOR CHRIST

The Apostles took the lead in preaching on the Day of Pentecost and thereafter, but the rapid growth of the Church was due to the fact that every Christian upon whom the Spirit came was from henceforth a witness for Christ, and an effective witness. Stephen was chosen as one of the deacons who should relieve the Apostles of the details of serving tables. This is recorded in the sixth chapter of Acts. In the seventh chapter, he had already become an eloquent preacher. Philip, another deacon, began a revival in the city of Samaria. (Acts 8:5.) Three times in Acts it is stated that the word of God increased, or continued to spread, and the number of the disciples multiplied. (Compare Acts 6:6 with Acts 12:24 and 19:20.)

We still need the preaching and leadership of ordained ministers just as the Early Church needed the preaching and leadership of the Apostles. But the Church will never have the power and influence so evident in the Early Church until every member again becomes a witness for his Saviour.

COURAGE AND CONFIDENCE

"Now when they saw the boldness of Peter and John, and perceived that they were unlearned and ignorant men, they marvelled; and they took knowledge of them, that they had been with Jesus." (Acts 4:13.) The transformation of the Apostles themselves, and of the other disciples, from the kind of men they were before Pentecost to the kind they were after Pentecost cannot be explained except by the fact that they had received power from on high. Thereafter, they stood before kings, councils, and courts without fear. With courage and confidence they gave their testimony everywhere they went. Men stopped to listen, "and the Lord added to the church daily such as should be saved." (Acts 2:47.)

Men still stop to hear those who speak with courage and confidence. The story is told of Voltaire that he was once met by a friend as he was hurrying on the streets of Paris. Asked where he was going, the French skeptic replied that he was on his way to hear a well-known street preacher. "What," exclaimed the friend, "you don't believe what he is preaching, do you?" "No," was the answer, "but he does, and I want to hear him say it."

The note of courage and confidence has too often been lacking in the words as well as in the lives of those who profess to be followers of Jesus. Only those are in the succession of the Apostles and the early Christians who know what they believe and cannot but speak the things they have seen and heard. (See Acts 4:20.)

FAITHFULNESS AND JOY

"And they [the disciples], continuing daily with one accord in the temple, and breaking bread from house to house, did eat their meat with gladness and singleness of heart." (Acts 2:46.) Every meal had become a sacrament to them, every experience an experience of God's saving power. No wonder they were faithful. No wonder they were filled with holy joy. No wonder they gave to every man who had need. No wonder they praised God and found favor with all the people. The Holy Spirit had come upon them, and that is what the Holy Spirit did for men of old. It is also what the Holy Spirit will do for Christians today if they will but let Him control their lives. "With the shock of a revelation it has come home to many [in our day] that God is not withholding Pentecosts, but that we are withstanding them."[36]

> "O Jehovah, I have heard the report of thee, and am afraid:
> O Jehovah, revive thy work in the midst of the years;
> In the midst of the years make it known."
>
> (HABAKKUK 3:2, A.S.V.)

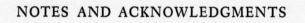

NOTES AND ACKNOWLEDGMENTS

Notes and Acknowledgments

1. Alfred, Lord Tennyson, "Flower in the Crannied Wall."
2. William G. T. Shedd, *A Critical and Doctrinal Commentary Upon the Epistle of St. Paul to the Romans* (Charles Scribner's Sons, 1879), p. 248.
3. *The Westminster Confession of Faith*, Chapter XII, Paragraph III.
4. Edward Mote, "My Hope Is Built on Nothing Less."
5. John Oxenham, in "The Cross at the Cross-ways," from *"Gentlemen — The King!"* Copyright in America by John Oxenham, and used by permission of Erica Oxenham.
6. George Croly, "Spirit of God, Descend Upon My Heart."
7. James Montgomery, "In the Hour of Trial."
8. Charles Hodge, *Commentary on the Epistle to the Romans* (Alfred Martien, Philadelphia, 1871), p. 419.
9. Phillips Brooks, *Addresses* (H. M. Caldwell Company, New York), pp. 17, 21.
10. Timothy Dwight, "I Love Thy Kingdom, Lord."
11. Sabine Baring-Gould, "Onward, Christian Soldiers."
12. Alfred North Whitehead, *Adventures of Ideas* (The Macmillan Company, 1933), p. 18.
13. Alexander Pope, "Essay on Man," Epistle II, Line 217.
14. Robert Robinson, "Come, Thou Fount of Every Blessing."
15. C. R. Vaughan, *The Gifts of the Holy Spirit to Unbelievers and Believers* (Presbyterian Committee of Publication, Richmond, Virginia, 1894), p. 266.
16. Isaac Watts, "Salvation! O the Joyful Sound."
17. John 17:3, R.S.V. (Italics ours.) This and other quotations from the Revised Standard Version of the New Testament are copyright, 1946, by the International Council of Religious Education, and used by permission.
18. Matthew Arnold, in "Immortality." Quoted in *Masterpieces of Religious Verse,* edited by James Dalton Morrison (Harper & Brothers, 1948), p. 601.
19. Paul Hamilton Hayne, "The True Heaven," from *Poems of Paul Hamilton Hayne* (D. Lothrop and Company, 1882).

20. Alexander Maclaren, *Expositions of Holy Scripture* (Ephesians), Volume XVI, p. 52.
21. Clara H. Scott, "Open My Eyes, That I May See." The Evangelical Publishing Company, Chicago, Copyright, 1895.
22. J. Armitage Robinson, *St. Paul's Epistle to the Ephesians*, Second Edition, p. 177. Copyright, 1903, by the Macmillan Company. Used by permission of the publishers.
23. *Ibid.*, p. 92.
24. F. W. Dillistone, *The Holy Spirit in the Life of Today* (The Westminster Press, 1947), p. 81.
25. Minutes of the General Assembly, Presbyterian Church, U. S., 1921. Appendix, pp. 189-190.
26. Harry Emerson Fosdick, *The Manhood of the Master* (Association Press, 1914), pp. 9-10.
27. James Denny, in *The Expositor's Bible*, Edited by W. Robertson Nicoll (Wm. B. Eerdmans Publishing Company, 1947), Vol. VI, p. 322.
28. G. A. Studdert-Kennedy, "Peace and Joy," from *The Sorrows of God.* Used by permission of Harper & Brothers.
29. William Wordsworth, "The World Is Too Much with Us."
30. Alexander Maclaren, in *The Expositor's Bible,* Edited by W. Robertson Nicoll, Vol. III, p. 140.
31. Latin, 11th Century, "Jesus, Thou Joy of Loving Hearts." Translated by Ray Palmer, 1858.
32. John M. Versteeg, *Perpetuating Pentecost* (Willett, Clark & Colby, 1930), p. 53.
33. F. B. Meyer. Quoted in *The Gospel According to St. John,* Edited by A. Plummer, Cambridge Greek Testament for Schools and Colleges (Cambridge University Press, 1913), p. 179.
34. Archer Butler, quoted in *The Ministry of the Spirit,* by A. J. Gordon (Fleming H. Revell Company, 1895), p. 133.
35. Bishop Webb, *The Presence and Office of the Spirit,* p. 47. Quoted in A. J. Gordon, *op. cit.,* p. 60 (footnote).
36. John M. Versteeg, *op. cit.,* Foreword.